HOW TO VALIDATE FEELINGS

A Comprehensive Blueprint To Acknowledge And Accept Your Emotions, Overcome Self Doubt Easily And Stop Second Guessing Yourself For Good!

Isabella Miguel

© **Copyright 2023 - All rights reserved.**

All rights reserved. No part of this guide may be reproduced, transmitted, or distributed in any form or by any means without permission in writing from the publisher except in the case of brief quotations embodied in critical articles or reviews.

Legal & Disclaimer

The content and information in this book are consistent and truthful, and it has been provided for informational, educational, and business purposes only.

Contents

Introduction 1

Chapter 1 4
The Development of Emotions

Chapter 2 18
Our Environment And Emotions

Chapter 3 31
Left Hemisphere Emotions

Chapter 4 51
The Right Hemisphere Emotions

Chapter 5 67
The Emotional Capacity of Love

Chapter 6 78
Serendipity

Chapter 7 92
Forgiveness

Chapter 8 107
Hope

Chapter 9 122
Pride

Chapter 10 134
Validating Your Feelings

Conclusion 143

Resources 146

Introduction

One of the greatest paradoxes of human existence is that we love to ask many questions even when we don't demand an honest answer. For instance, we often ask people, "How are you feeling?" as though we really care about their emotional health. Questions like this make us assume we attach so much importance to our emotional health, even when we don't really care as much as we do for our physical health. Somehow, our emotional health has not been a matter of great concern for us, just as we do for our physical health. But if we look deeply, we will understand that how we feel inside influences how we feel outside. In other words, our emotions influence actions and behavior.

The reason why it's been hard for many people to stay in control of their life is that they've not been able to gain control over their emotions. Someone who finds it hard or has not mastered the art of discarding negative feelings (left hemisphere) and replacing them with positive feelings (right hemisphere) might not be able to make quality decisions that can affect their lives positively.

Emotions are powerful. They are the forces behind our decisions. They can tell how far we go in life and what kind of people and energy we attract. But one unfortunate thing is that we don't talk about it as much as we do about our physical health. In fact, most of us tend to dismiss our emotional health. We certainly don't discuss it at the office, around the dinner table, or really anywhere. Instead, we find it convenient to chat about our physical wellness - the kind of food we eat, the type of exercise we try and do not try to do, how and when we sleep or not to. The truth is handling life issues might really be difficult without a better way to handle emotions. When you have a healthy attitude about emotions and know how they can be expressed, you will be better equipped to handle the ups and downs of life. But when the reserve is the case. You are more likely to face stress, depression, anxiety, and other mental health issues.

Since we don't experience different emotions the same way, it would be best if you have a better understanding of your own feelings as a person. This will help you recognize your feelings, acknowledge them, and take a drastic step towards changing negative ones and, by doing so, improve your quality of life.

Take this book as a resourceful material that will help you ease the journey to figure out your emotions. The book is packed with adequate information on how to validate your feelings, control your emotions, and overcome negative thoughts that can hinder you from becoming productive.

In this book, you will learn various developmental stages of emotions, how your environment influences your emotions, and some tips you can implement to get your emotions in good shape.

Let's get started!

Chapter 1

The Development of Emotions

Emotions are like a roller coaster ride - One minute, you feel elated and like a king, and the next minute you feel sad and discouraged. But what exactly are emotions? Emotions are an integral aspect of our lives - they shape how we feel, think, and behave. They can be described as feelings that arise in response to a particular situation or event.

For example, imagine walking down the street and seeing a cute puppy. Your initial reaction might be joy and excitement - after all, who doesn't love puppies? But if you've had a negative experience with a dog in the past, your emotions might quickly shift to fear or anxiety. But despite their unpredictability and complexity, emotions are essential to the human experience. They allow us to connect with others, make decisions, and navigate the ups and downs of life.

Elements of Emotions

Have you ever wondered why you feel certain when encountering certain situations or people? Emotions are complex, and a combination of various elements forms them. Understanding the components of emotions can help you gain a deeper insight into how and why you feel the way you do. This section will explore the three key components of emotions: subjective experience, physiological response, and behavioural response. We'll dive into each element, unpacking how they work together to create the widest range of emotions we experience daily. By the end of this section, you'll have a clearer understanding of how your emotions are formed. So, let's get started!

Subjective experience

Picture this: you're at a restaurant with a friend, and they tell you a joke that you find hilarious. You burst out laughing, tears streaming down your face. But if someone else had told you the same joke at a different time, you might have barely cracked a smile. That's because emotions are highly subjective - they're influenced by a wide range of factors, including our mood, past experiences, and current environment.

Take anger, for instance. While we might label all angry feelings as "anger," the reality is much more complex. Your own experience of anger might range from a mild annoyance to an all-consuming rage, depending on the situation and your personal history.

And emotions don't always occur in isolation. We might experience a complex mix of emotions in response to a particular event or situation. For example, starting a new job might bring up feelings of both excitement and nervousness. Getting married or having a child might trigger several emotions, from joy and excitement to anxiety and fear.

Physiological responses

When you feel a strong emotion, it's not just something that's happening in your head - it's also having a physical impact on your body. For example, you might notice your heart racing or your palms getting sweaty.

The sympathetic nervous system, a part of your nervous system, regulates these physical responses. This system controls involuntary responses like blood flow and digestion and plays a key role in your body's fight-or-flight reactions.

So, when you're facing a threat or danger, your body automatically prepares to either run away or confront the threat head-on. This can trigger an array of physical reactions, including increased heart rate, rapid breathing, and even shaking.

But while early studies on the physiology of emotion focused mainly on these autonomic responses, more recent research has shown that the brain also plays a critical role in emotions. In particular, the amygdala - a small, almond-shaped structure in the limbic system - has been shown to be involved in fear and other strong emotions.

For instance, the amygdala becomes activated when people are shown threatening images. And damage to the amygdala can impair your ability to feel fear.

So, while emotions may feel like they're happening entirely in your head, they're having a powerful impact on your whole body.

Behavioural response

When we experience emotions, it doesn't just happen within us - it's also something that we express outwardly. The way we express our emotions can be just as important as the emotions themselves, and it can significantly impact the people around us.

Many emotional expressions are universal. For example, a smile indicates happiness, while a frown indicates sadness. This means that people all over the world can interpret these expressions in a similar way, regardless of their culture or background.

But at the same time, sociocultural norms can also affect how we express and interpret emotions. In some cultures, it may be more acceptable to express negative emotions openly, while in others, it may be more common to mask these emotions in the presence of authority figures or strangers.

Overall, our ability to accurately interpret emotional expressions is linked to our emotional intelligence. This involves not only recognizing and understanding our own emotions but also being able to pick up on the emotions of others and respond appropriately.

How emotions affect us

Imagine waking up every morning feeling a deep sense of sadness that seems to weigh you down. You go through your day with a heavy heart, unable to shake off the feeling of despair. This is the reality for many people who struggle with their emotions on a daily basis. The impact of our emotions can be far-reaching, affecting our personal well-being and overall quality of life.

Let's take a look at Dorcas. Dorcas had been struggling with depression for years, and it seemed to be getting worse. She found it difficult to get out of bed in the morning and didn't have the energy to do much during the day. Her sadness seemed to permeate every aspect of her life, including her relationships with her children.

Even though she loved them deeply, Dorcas found it challenging to connect with her kids. She often felt like she was just going through the motions of parenting rather than being fully present and engaged. Her children noticed this distance and began to withdraw from her in turn. Dorcas's sadness was affecting her own life and those of her children.

So that we don't end up being like Dorcas, we will explore how emotions affect us and the different ways they can impact our lives in this section. Let's proceed.

Physical health

Did you know that emotions can significantly impact your physical health? It's true! Negative emotions like chronic anxiety, constant dwelling in the past, or displaying hostile behaviour patterns can all put you at risk for a range of health problems.

For instance, if you're someone who experiences negative emotions frequently, you might be at risk for cardiovascular disease, asthma, hypertension, and more. Research has shown that a depressive mood can lead to significant changes in your cellular immunity, including lower lymphocyte response to antigens, reduced natural killer cell activity, and fewer white cells in your blood.

Unfortunately, when you experience unhealthy emotions like chronic stress, hostility, or depression, your immune system can become dysregulated, which can lead to inflammation in your body. This can result in various health problems, including cardiovascular disease, osteoporosis, type 2 diabetes, arthritis, certain cancers, and even frailty.

On the other hand, a positive outlook on life can significantly impact your physical health. Having a positive outlook has been linked to lower blood pressure, better weight control, reduced cardiovascular risk, healthy blood sugar levels, and increased longevity. It's amazing how our emotional state can impact different aspects of our health, from our cardiovascular system to our immune function and endocrine physiology.

Decision-making

When you want to make decisions, do you rely on your intuition, or do you take a logical approach? The truth is, even if you think you're being rational, your emotions are often guiding your decision-making process. By understanding the role emotions play in our decision-making, we can learn to strike a balance between reason and intuition and make choices that align with our goals and values.

Emotions are created when our brains interpret the events and situations around us based on our memories, thoughts, and beliefs. This triggers how we feel and behave, influencing all our decisions in some way. Emotional decision-making is natural and happens unconsciously, whether we're aware of it or not.

For example, if you are happy, you might decide to take a stroll through a sunny park. But if you had a traumatic experience with a dog as a child, that same park might trigger feelings of fear, leading you to take the bus instead. Logical arguments can be made for both choices, but ultimately, the decision is driven by your emotional state.

Different emotions affect decisions in different ways. Sadness, for instance, can make you more willing to settle for less, such as not putting yourself forward for a promotion or staying in a toxic relationship. On the flip side, sadness can also make you more generous and empathetic toward others.

Anger, on the other hand, can lead to impatience and hasty decision-making. When you're excited, you might make quick decisions without considering the long-term implications, driven by confidence and optimism about the future. And if you're feeling afraid, your decisions may be clouded by uncertainty and caution, leading you to take longer to make a choice.

While your gut feeling is an important part of the decision-making process, it can sometimes lead you astray, resulting in poor judgment, bias, recklessness, or risk aversion. That's why you must be aware of your emotional state and take a step back and evaluate your options before making a decision.

Productivity

Have you ever had a day at work where your emotions were all over the place? Maybe you woke up feeling grumpy, got stuck in traffic on your way to the office, and then found out that you had a big project due that day. It's no secret that emotions can have a significant impact on our productivity at work.

When you have positive emotions, such as pride and enthusiasm, you're more likely to feel motivated and energized to tackle your tasks. These feelings can lead to increased job satisfaction and productivity. Conversely, negative emotions, such as stress, anxiety, and resentment, can make it difficult to focus and stay motivated.

For instance, when you feel appreciated, you are more likely to experience positive emotions, which can lead to increased motivation and productivity. On the other hand, if you feel unsupported or undervalued, you may experience negative emotions that can lead to decreased motivation and productivity.

Relationships with others

Have you ever noticed how your emotions can affect the way you interact with others? Whether it's through words, facial expressions, or body language, our emotions are constantly communicating information to those around us. But did you know that emotions also have an interpersonal function that can influence our social interactions?

When we express our emotions, we send signals to others about how we feel and what our intentions are. These signals can help others understand our interpersonal relationships and the environment we are in. For example, a smile and a warm embrace can signal happiness and affection in a romantic relationship, while a frown and crossed arms can signal anger and disapproval.

Because emotions have signal value, they can help us solve social problems by evoking responses from others. For instance, if you're feeling sad and expressing it, your friends might comfort you, offer you support or space, or just sit with you quietly, depending on what they think you need. Similarly, expressing joy might encourage your friends to celebrate with you or join in your excitement.

Emotions also provide incentives for desired social behaviour. For example, expressing gratitude towards someone who has helped you in some way can encourage that person to continue to help you in the future. Or, expressing anger towards someone who has treated you unfairly can motivate them to change their behaviour.

Creativity

Do you know that emotions affect your creativity? Well, positive emotional states, like feeling happy, can enhance your creative thinking. However, this boost is short-lived, and the effect is small, meaning that there is more to the role of emotions in creativity than we previously thought.

For example, positive activated moods like happiness can boost your creative idea generation by broadening your attention. Creative divergent thinking can also be enhanced through open-monitoring meditation and mind wandering as emotion regulation processes.

Interestingly, negative activating moods like anger can also stimulate the exploration of ideas, especially if you're angry about something outside of work, like systemic injustices. However, if you're angry about something directly related to your job, it could lead to dark creativity, such as harmful actions towards others or the organization.

In addition, managing your emotions through emotion regulation processes is also important in maintaining effort and persistence. Three sets of emotional regulation processes that might be especially relevant are managing affected intensity, managing appraisals, and managing resources.

Lastly, your personal attributes, like your gender, can also influence both your affective experiences and your creativity.

Women tend to have less support for creativity, which predicts their creative behaviour at work.

Difference Between Emotions and Feelings

Imagine sitting at a coffee shop, sipping your drink, and scrolling through your social media feed. Suddenly, you come across a post that triggers a strong emotional response. Your heart rate increases, and you feel a knot in your stomach. You might label this feeling as anger or frustration. But did you know that the feeling you're experiencing is a reaction to the emotion that was triggered by the post?

Let's break it down a bit further. Emotions are automatic responses to external stimuli, such as the post you saw on social media. They originate from the amygdala, which is part of your brain responsible for processing emotions. Now, once you perceive this external stimulus, your brain processes it, and you experience an emotion. However, it's important to note that this emotional response doesn't always result in a conscious feeling.

Feelings, on the other hand, are the conscious experience of emotions. They arise when your brain assigns meaning to your emotional experience. For instance, you may feel angry or frustrated after seeing the post, but these feelings are subjective and vary from person to person. Additionally, feelings can become even more specific than emotional responses and may be brought up from physical reactions to different things like hunger or pain.

So, while emotions and feelings may seem similar, they are distinct from each other. Emotions are automatic and can occur without conscious awareness, while feelings are conscious experiences that are derived from emotions. It's important to understand this distinction because it can help you manage your emotions and regulate your feelings effectively.

In conclusion, emotions are important in our daily lives, and they can have a significant impact on our overall well-being. Understanding what emotions are, how they are formed, and their effects on us can help us better manage them and improve our lives.

Key Takeaways

- Our emotions are subjective to the circumstances around us.

- Our body physiology also plays a key role in our emotions.

- Our emotional state can impact different aspects of our health.

- Emotions also impact our decision-making ability.
- Emotions and Feelings are different yet intertwined.

Chapter 2

Our Environment And Emotions

Have you ever noticed how your environment can impact your emotions? Perhaps you've felt more stressed than usual after spending time in a cluttered, disorganized space. Or maybe you feel a sense of calm when surrounded by nature. These experiences are not just in your head – there are real and powerful links between your environment and your emotions.

Research has shown that living in a dirty, messy home can be damaging to your emotional well-being. It creates chaos and clutter when your mind craves order and stability. Similarly, the type of city you live in can also make a difference. People who reside in polluted or dangerous areas tend to have lower emotional wellness scores than those who live in happy, productive, and clean locations.

Of course, each person is unique, and what affects one person emotionally might not affect another in the same way. That being said, multiple environmental factors can play a role in our emotional health. Whether it's the colours in our environment, the noise level, or the amount of natural light we receive, our surroundings have a profound impact on how we feel.

Consider the following example: Imagine that you're in a dark, windowless room with no natural light. You might start to feel anxious or claustrophobic after a while. Now, imagine that you're in a bright, airy space with plenty of natural light. You might feel more energized and optimistic in this environment.

The bottom line is that our environment and our emotions are not separate entities – they are deeply intertwined. By understanding how our surroundings affect our emotions, we can take steps to create a more positive and uplifting environment for ourselves. In the upcoming chapters, we'll explore the various ways in which environmental factors impact our emotions and how to create a more supportive and nurturing environment.

Environmental factors that influence our emotions

There are many factors that affect our emotional state, from the colour of the walls to the level of noise. Here, we will explore some of the specific environmental factors that can influence our perceptions and interpretations and ultimately impact our emotions. Let's proceed.

Familiarity

Have you ever noticed how familiar surroundings can impact how you feel? Perhaps you feel a sense of comfort and relaxation when you return to your childhood home or your favourite local coffee shop. On the other hand, maybe you feel anxious or uneasy when you're in a place that reminds you of a difficult or painful experience.

It turns out that the level of familiarity we have with our environment can have a powerful impact on our emotions. When we have positive associations with a space, we tend to feel more at ease and connected to it. This is why going home to our parent's house or visiting a childhood vacation spot can feel like a balm for the soul.

However, familiarity can also be a double-edged sword. If we associate space with negative experiences, it can be difficult to shake those feelings even if the environment itself has changed. This is why going back to a place where you were once mistreated or unhappy can be a triggering experience.

The good news is that we can adjust the level of familiarity in our environment to better suit our emotional needs. If we want to create a sense of comfort and familiarity in our home, we might add personal touches such as photo mementoes that remind us of happy memories. On the other hand, if we find that certain items or objects are causing us distress, we can choose to remove them or put them out of sight.

Ultimately, the relationship between familiarity and our emotions is complex and highly individual. What brings comfort and joy to one person may trigger negative feelings in another.

People

One day, Maria woke up feeling energized and excited about her upcoming day. She had plans to meet up with a group of friends for a day of hiking and outdoor adventure, and she couldn't wait to spend time with them.

However, when she arrived at the hiking trailhead, she found that one of her friends had brought along a new acquaintance who Maria had never met before. From the moment they started hiking, Maria felt like this person was a negative presence – constantly complaining, criticizing the trail, and making snide comments about the group's plans.

Despite the beauty of the natural surroundings and the company of her other friends, Maria found that she couldn't shake this negative feeling. By the end of the day, she felt exhausted, discouraged, and drained of her initial enthusiasm.

This experience showed Maria how much the people we spend time with can impact our emotions. Even when we're in a beautiful, inspiring environment, the presence of one negative person can completely shift our perspective and leave us feeling drained and depleted. Conversely, when we surround ourselves with positive, supportive individuals, we can feel uplifted and energized, even in the face of difficult circumstances.

This is why it's so important to be careful about who we share our spaces with. When we cultivate low-conflict, compassionate relationships with people who lift us up, we create a supportive environment that can help to bolster our emotional well-being. These relationships don't always have to be exciting or flashy – sometimes, it's the quiet moments of shared support and understanding that can make the biggest difference.

Of course, it's not always possible to completely avoid negative or unsupportive people in our lives. We may have family members, coworkers, or acquaintances who bring us down, despite our best efforts to stay positive. In these situations, it's important to set healthy boundaries and prioritize our own well-being. This might mean limiting our time around these individuals or seeking out additional support from friends, family members, or mental health professionals.

Senses

When you walk into a room, you might feel an immediate shift in your mood. Or you feel instantly calm and relaxed or feel agitated and restless. This is because our senses are constantly taking in information from our environment and feeding it back to our brains, influencing our emotional state.

One key factor in this equation is lighting. Exposure to sunlight during the day can help regulate our circadian rhythms and promote feelings of alertness and energy, while dimmer lighting can help us wind down and relax in the evening. That's why companies that specialize in window treatments, like shutters, often take light control very seriously. By adjusting the amount and type of light that enters a room, they can help create a more optimal environment for emotional well-being.

Smell is another powerful sense that can impact our emotions. Certain scents, like lavender or peppermint, have been shown to have calming effects, while others, like citrus or rosemary, can promote energy and focus. Experimenting with different scents in your environment can be a fun and effective way to influence your emotional state.

Finally, noise pollution can also be a significant factor in how we feel in a given space. Whether it's the sound of traffic outside your window or the constant hum of machinery in a nearby building, unwanted noises can be a major source of stress and agitation. That's why many people choose to install sound insulation or white noise machines to help block out noises and create a more peaceful, tranquil environment.

Culture

Culture can have a profound impact on your emotions. From the way you express yourself to the way you deal with stress, your culture plays a significant role in shaping your emotional experiences. For example, in some cultures, expressing emotions openly and freely is encouraged, while in others, it may be seen as inappropriate or even taboo.

In addition to this, cultural norms can also influence how you cope with difficult situations. For instance, some cultures value stoicism and encourage individuals to suppress their emotions in challenging times, while others promote seeking social support and expressing emotions to cope with stress.

Moreover, cultural practices and traditions can have a direct impact on your emotional well-being. The food you eat, the music you listen to, and the rituals you follow can all influence your mood and emotions. For instance, participating in cultural celebrations or religious ceremonies can evoke feelings of joy and connection, while consuming comfort food from your culture can bring a sense of familiarity and comfort during difficult times.

What should I do?

I recently had a conversation with a woman who was struggling with her emotions. She told me how her cluttered home and toxic relationships were making her feel anxious and drained. As we talked, I shared with her two pieces of advice that could help her regain control and improve her emotions. If you're also feeling overwhelmed by your environment, I'd like to share these tips with you too.

Adapt

When faced with an environment that influences your emotions, it's important to remember that you have the power to adapt. Although it may be easier to change your physical environment, you can also make changes to your thoughts, emotions, and behaviour. Think of the obstacles in your environment as immovable objects that you can use as stepping stones to reach your goals. By managing your response to these obstacles, you can create a healthier and more positive environment for yourself.

One way to adapt is by setting healthy personal boundaries. If you have a boss who is dictatorial, for example, you can set boundaries by speaking up for yourself and communicating your needs. Learning to say "no" to unreasonable demands can help you maintain your mental and emotional health. You can also work on managing your emotions and thoughts in response to difficult situations. Instead of reacting impulsively, try to pause and reflect on the situation before responding.

Remember, adapting doesn't mean settling for less or choosing to be powerless. It means recognizing your own agency and taking action to create a better environment for yourself.

Focus on what you can control.

Changing your environment can have a significant impact on your emotional state. However, it's essential to focus on what you can control and not feel overwhelmed by the things that are beyond your control.

If your environment is cluttered or disorganized, taking steps to tidy up can create a sense of calm and order that can positively impact your mood. Similarly, adjusting your relationships by spending time with people who uplift you and avoiding those who drain your energy can also have a significant impact on your emotional well-being.

Of course, there are some things that are outside of your control, such as crime rates in your area. In these cases, it's important to take steps to ensure your safety and well-being but also recognize that you can't change everything.

Change your perceptive

Do you feel like the world is out to get you? Like, no matter what you do, things just don't seem to go your way. Well, have you considered that maybe it's not the world that's the problem but rather your perception of it?

By modifying how you see things, you can have a huge impact on your emotions. If you're always on high alert, expecting danger at every turn, then it's no wonder you're constantly on edge. But if you can shift your focus to the positive opportunities around you and not take yourself too seriously, you might just find yourself flourishing.

Another helpful strategy is forming a routine. When you have a daily structure in place, it can create a sense of control in your life, which can be incredibly calming. Plus, it gives you the space and freedom to pursue the things that really matter to you without feeling overwhelmed or lost.

So, if you feel like the world is against you, try adjusting your perceptions and forming a routine. You might just find that things start falling into place a little more easily.

Hemisphere of Emotions

Left Hemisphere   Right Hemisphere

No, it is not another science class. It's a pictorial representation of the two hemispheres of emotions. Don't worry; it's not anything complicated; let me explain.

Emotions are complex and multifaceted experiences that are processed by different parts of the brain. Our emotions can be divided into two categories, based on the brain's hemispheres responsible for processing them: right-hemisphere emotions and left-hemisphere emotions.

Right-hemisphere emotions are often associated with positive feelings, such as joy, happiness, and love. This is because the brain's right hemisphere is responsible for processing nonverbal information, such as facial expressions, tone of voice, and body language. It helps us to perceive and understand the emotional cues of others, which in turn allows us to form social connections and experience positive emotions.

On the other hand, left-hemisphere emotions are often associated with negative feelings, such as anger, sadness, and fear. This is because the brain's left hemisphere is responsible for processing verbal and analytical information, such as language, logic, and reasoning. It helps us to interpret and analyze the world around us, but it can also lead us to overthink and ruminate on negative experiences, which can trigger negative emotions.

Of course, emotions are not as simple as just being in the right or left hemisphere. The brain is a complex and dynamic organ, and various factors, including genetics, environment, and life experiences, influence emotions. Nevertheless, understanding the basic differences between right-hemisphere emotions and left-hemisphere emotions can help us to better understand our emotional experiences and how our brains process them.

In conclusion, it's crucial to identify the impact our environment can have on our emotions. While we can't always have control over external factors, we have the power to choose how we respond to them. By creating a positive and supportive physical and social environment and learning to adapt and manage our thoughts and emotions, we can cultivate a sense of calm and well-being in our lives. Remember, a healthy environment equals a healthy mind.

Key Takeaways

- Multiple environmental factors can play a role in our emotional health.

- Emotions can be divided into the right and left hemispheres.

- Our senses play a major role in our emotions.

- Changing your environment can have a significant impact on your emotional state.

- By modifying how you see things, you can have a huge impact on your emotions.

Chapter 3

Left Hemisphere Emotions

Have you ever experienced emotions that seem to take over your mind and body, leaving you feeling overwhelmed and unable to control your reactions? These emotions are often categorized as left-hemisphere emotions, as we discussed earlier. They are reactions to stressors, both real and perceived, and can have a profound impact on our well-being. That is why I have dedicated this chapter to exploring some left-hemisphere emotions and the effect it has on you. This chapter is important because you might not know that you experience or express these emotions. So, it's best that you know what they are so that you will be able to overcome them. Let's proceed.

Anger

Anger is a normal and natural emotion that arises when we interpret and react to certain situations. Every individual has their own set of triggers that can cause them to feel angry, but some common ones include feeling threatened, frustrated, powerless, invalidated, or treated unfairly.

It's important to remember that people can interpret situations differently, so what makes you angry might not necessarily make someone else angry. For example, one person might find it amusing when someone cuts in front of them in line, while another person might feel very angry and upset about it.

It's also important to know that just because you get angry about something, it doesn't mean you're interpreting the situation 'wrong.' Your feelings and reactions are valid, and it's important to acknowledge and express them in a healthy way.

For instance, instead of yelling or getting physical, you could take deep breaths, count to ten, or even step away from the situation for a moment to cool off.

Now, when we experience anger in a healthy way, it can be really helpful. This is what we call adaptive anger. It's like a signal telling us that something isn't quite right and needs to be addressed. And once we take action to fix the problem, the anger tends to fade away pretty quickly, usually in about 20 minutes.

However, sometimes our anger can become maladaptive. This means that it's not productive and can cause more harm than good. For example, if we hold onto our anger for too long, it can start to build up and cause all sorts of issues, like headaches and even depression. And if we use anger as our only way of feeling powerful or safe, it can lead to problems in our relationships with others.

But do you know that anger is in stages? Yes, it is. Anger doesn't just happen; it passes through a process. Here are the stages of anger.

Buildup

This is where the foundation of anger is laid, and it's an important stage because it can give us clues as to why we're feeling angry in the first place.

The buildup of anger can be caused by a variety of factors, including negative thoughts and attitudes about ourselves, others, or our environment. For example, if we're constantly thinking pessimistically about the past or the future, or if we have low self-esteem or a negative view of our own abilities, this can contribute to the buildup of anger.

As this buildup continues, it can start to manifest itself physically. You might notice yourself sweating, clenching your fists, or frowning and scowling. These physical signs of stress are a way for your body to show that something is not quite right and that you might need to address the underlying issue before the anger grows and becomes even more intense.

So, if you find yourself experiencing the buildup stage of anger, it's important to take a step back and try to identify the root cause of your feelings. By doing so, you can address the issue before it becomes overwhelming and leads to more serious problems.

Spark

The spark represents something that sets off an outburst of anger. It can be either internal or external, but it's always a product of the buildup of anger that we talked about earlier.

Internally, the spark can come from a child's own thoughts and feelings. For example, they might think negative thoughts about themselves or their environment, and these thoughts can quickly turn into angry, physical responses like throwing things or breaking things.

Externally, the spark might come from someone else's actions or words. For example, if someone says something hurtful to a child, this could ignite their anger and cause them to lash out in response.

To give you an example, let's say two children are playing a game that requires a competitive drive. One child grew up in a household where they were constantly told that winning was everything and losing made them feel inferior and unworthy. The other children grew up in a more supportive environment, where they were encouraged to do their best regardless of the outcome.

If the first child loses the game, their expectations and low self-esteem act as the spark that ignites their anger, causing them to react in a negative way. On the other hand, if the second child loses, they might be disappointed, but they'll be able to move on without getting angry because they've been taught to focus on the effort they put in rather than the outcome.

The Explosion

The third stage of anger is the explosion, where a person's anger reaches its peak and explodes outward in a burst of aggressive behaviour. This stage is often accompanied by yelling, screaming, physical violence, or other intense expressions of anger. It's important to note that during this stage, the person displaying their anger might not be in full control of their actions or be aware of the harm they're causing to others.

For example, let's say Mike is at his best friend's birthday party, and he sees his friend's parents showering him with love and affection. This can trigger a spark of anger in Mike because he never received this type of support from his own parents. As the party goes on, someone asks Mike about his own parents, and he responds with curses and flips over a table, causing a scene.

This type of explosion of anger can have negative consequences for the person displaying it and those around them.

The aftermath

Once the anger has subsided, it's crucial to address any issues that arose during the previous stages. This is known as the aftermath stage, where you need to engage in problem-solving and communication to prevent any harm to yourself or others. Failure to address the underlying issues that caused the buildup and spark of anger may result in repeated outbursts of anger, leading to more harm than good.

Fear

Fear is another left-hemisphere emotion that's worth taking note of. Have you ever felt your heart racing, your palms sweating, and your breathing becoming shallow when you encounter something scary or dangerous? That's fear in action. Fear is a primal emotion that warns us of the presence of danger or the threat of harm, whether physical or psychological.

Sometimes fear is justified, but other times it can be irrational and stem from imagined dangers. It's a natural response to some situations, but it can also be overwhelming and disrupt our lives when extreme or out of proportion to the actual threat.

Fear can sometimes be a sign of a mental health condition, including panic disorder, social anxiety disorder, phobias, and post-traumatic stress disorder (PTSD).

When we sense a threat, our bodies react in a variety of ways, including sweating, increased heart rate, and high adrenaline levels, which prepare us to fight or flee. This response is known as the "fight or flight" response.

The emotional response to fear, however, is unique to each individual and may depend on past experiences, beliefs, and values. Some people enjoy feeling scared, like when they watch horror movies or participate in extreme sports. For others, fear is something to be avoided at all costs, and they may experience a negative emotional response to fear-inducing situations.

Symptoms of fear may vary, but some common symptoms include chest pain, dry mouth, rapid heartbeat, nausea, sweating, shortness of breath, trembling, feeling overwhelmed, an upset stomach, and a sense of impending death.

Resentment

Have you ever felt that pang of bitterness and anger when you feel wronged by someone? That's resentment. It's a negative emotional reaction to feeling mistreated or wronged by another person. It's a normal feeling to experience frustration and disappointment in life, but when these feelings are too overwhelming, they can lead to resentment.

Resentment is a complex mix of emotions, including anger, disappointment, bitterness, and hard feelings. It's like a heavy weight that you carry around with you, affecting not only your emotional state but also your relationships. When you're harbouring resentment, it's difficult to trust and love someone fully, and it can cause damage that's sometimes irreparable, just like it affected Deborah.

Deborah was a bright young lady who had always excelled in school and had big dreams for her future. However, with time, she started to feel resentful towards her family and friends, who she felt weren't supporting her dreams or taking her goals seriously. She felt like she was always being overlooked or underestimated, and this made her angry and frustrated.

This resentment started to affect her relationships, as she became increasingly distant and withdrawn from those around her. She stopped confiding in her friends and family and began to isolate herself from social events and activities. She also started to doubt herself, wondering if maybe she wasn't as talented or capable as she had thought.

This self-doubt then reinforced her resentment as she became even more convinced that no one believed in her or appreciated her talents. She stopped putting effort into her schoolwork and stopped pursuing her passions, as she felt like it wasn't worth it if no one else cared.

The reality is that there's no one cause for resentment, but there are common triggers that often lead to these feelings. For example, relationships with people who always insist on being right, being taken advantage of by someone, feeling put down, or having unrealistic expectations of others are common triggers for resentment.

Do you have a friend who always seems to talk over you and dismiss your ideas? Or perhaps you've been in a situation where you feel like you're doing all the work, but someone else takes all the credit. These are examples of situations that can trigger resentment.

Interestingly, people who experienced resentment might not know. Here are some signs of resentment to look out for.

Recurrent reply to the event

When you feel resentful towards someone, it's not uncommon for your mind to replay the event that caused the resentment over and over again. It's like a broken record that you can't turn off. You may find yourself constantly ruminating about the situation and the actions of the person who wronged you.

The more you think about the situation, the more intense the resentment can become, which only further perpetuates the cycle of negative thoughts. It's like a snowball effect that can quickly spiral out of control.

Feeling of regret

When you hold onto resentment, you may start to dwell on past events and wish that things could have been different. This can cause feelings of regret and remorse to arise. You may blame yourself for not handling the situation differently, even if there was nothing you could have done to change the outcome.

These feelings of regret can cause you to feel stuck in the past, unable to move on from the event that caused you to feel mistreated or wronged. Instead of focusing on the present moment and creating positive experiences for yourself, you may find yourself trapped in a cycle of negative thoughts and self-blame.

Avoidance or fear

When you feel resentment towards someone or a situation, it can create fear or avoidance in you. You may start to fear interacting with certain people or situations that bring up negative emotions. These unwanted memories of wrongdoing can be painful to think about, and it's natural to want to protect yourself from experiencing those emotions again.

For example, if you feel resentful towards a friend who betrayed your trust, you may avoid spending time with them or other friends who remind you of the situation. This avoidance may provide temporary relief from negative emotions, but it can also prevent you from healing and moving forward.

Similarly, if you feel resentful towards a certain situation, you may avoid it altogether. For instance, if you feel resentment towards a particular job or workplace, you may avoid applying for similar positions or even avoid going to work altogether.

Frustration

Frustration is an emotional response to stress, which can arise from various situations, such as work-related stress, the pursuit of unattainable goals, and the inability to find solutions to problems. It is a common feeling that everyone experiences at some point in their lives. However, being in a constant state of frustration can lead to left-hemisphere emotions and affect one's mental health.

When you are unable to achieve a goal despite putting in the effort, it can lead to feelings of irritability or anger, which are characteristic of frustration. If this feeling persists, it can lead to a loss of confidence, stress, anger, aggressive behaviour, irritability, and even depression. For instance, if you are working towards a promotion but keep getting passed over for it, the frustration you feel can lead to negative emotions that affect your overall well-being.

Frustration can be broadly categorized into two types: internal and external frustration. Internal frustration occurs when you are dissatisfied with yourself or your reaction to a situation. You might be unhappy with the way you handled a particular event or regret not having made a different choice. External frustration, on the other hand, is caused by a stressor that originates outside of you. This could be a physical object or a situation that creates an obstacle to achieving a goal or reaching a desired outcome. Examples of external frustration include traffic jams, long wait times, or dealing with a difficult boss or coworker. By identifying the source of frustration, you can better understand how to cope with it and work towards finding a solution.

Anxiety

Jerry had always been a nervous person, but as he grew older, his anxiety began to take over his life. Every little thing would set him off, and he constantly worried about the future. One day, Jerry had to give a big presentation at work. He had prepared for weeks, but as the day approached, he felt his anxiety building. On the day of the presentation, Jerry's heart was pounding, and his palms were sweating. He couldn't focus on anything except his fear of messing up.

During the presentation, Jerry stumbled over his words and lost his place on the slides. He felt like a failure and was sure that everyone in the room was judging him. After the presentation, he couldn't stop replaying the mistakes he had made and worrying about the future consequences. Jerry's experience shows how anxiety can take over a person's thoughts and emotions.

Anxiety is something that many people experience, and it can be really tough to deal with. When you're feeling anxious, your body is reacting to a perceived threat, even if the threat isn't there, just like in the case of Jerry. Your brain releases adrenaline, which triggers a fight-or-flight response. That's why you might feel like you're on high alert or you're ready to run away from something.

The physical symptoms of anxiety can be really uncomfortable, too. You might feel like your heart is racing or like you're sweating a lot. Some people even feel like they're going to pass out or throw up. These symptoms can make it hard to focus on anything else, and they can make you feel really out of control.

How Left Hemisphere Emotions Lead to Self-Doubt

Left-hemisphere emotions can have a powerful impact on our thoughts and behaviours, often leading to self-doubt and undermining our confidence. When we experience left-hemisphere emotions such as fear, anger, anxiety, frustration, or resentment, they can trigger a range of cognitive and emotional responses that contribute to self-doubt. In this section, we will explore some of the ways in which left-hemisphere emotions can lead to self-doubt. Let's proceed.

Magnifying flaws

When you experience negative emotions such as anger or frustration, it's common for your mind to focus on your flaws or mistakes, which can create feelings of inadequacy. For example, let's say you made a mistake at work that cost the company some money, and your boss was angry with you. If you focus on that mistake and feel frustrated or angry with yourself, you might start to doubt your abilities and worry that you're not good enough at your job. This can lead to vicious self-doubt, where you're constantly questioning your abilities and feeling anxious or insecure.

Similarly, if you experience fear or anxiety, you might start to magnify your flaws or weaknesses in order to protect yourself from potential threats or failures. For instance, if you're afraid of public speaking, you might focus on all the ways in which you're not a good speaker, which can make you feel even more nervous and self-conscious. In these cases, it's important to recognize that left-hemisphere emotions can create a distorted view of yourself and your abilities.

Limited perspective

When you experience left-hemisphere emotions like resentment or disappointment, it can be challenging to see the positive aspects of a situation. In fact, it can limit your perspective, causing you to focus only on the negative aspects of a situation and ignore the positives. This can be especially damaging when it comes to your self-image, as you may begin to doubt your own abilities or worth based solely on your left hemisphere emotions. For instance, let's say you received some constructive criticism on a project you worked hard on, and you feel disappointed that your work wasn't perfect. If you focus solely on your disappointment and don't take into account the fact that you still completed the project successfully, you may start to doubt your abilities as a professional or even as a person. This narrow perspective can cause you to overlook your strengths and accomplishments, leading to feelings of inadequacy and self-doubt.

Loss of confidence

Left-hemisphere emotions like anxiety can slowly chip away at your confidence over time. When you experience left hemisphere emotions frequently or for extended periods, it's easy to start questioning your abilities and feeling less capable or competent than you really are. For instance, if you're feeling anxious about an upcoming presentation, you might start to doubt your public speaking abilities, which can lead to a loss of confidence. Similarly, if you're feeling frustrated with your progress on a project, you might start to question your skills and abilities, which can cause your confidence to falter. Over time, this loss of confidence can become a self-fulfilling prophecy, as you may begin to avoid situations that require you to use the skills you doubt, further reinforcing your negative beliefs about yourself.

Self-criticism

Left-hemisphere emotions can lead to an increase in self-critical thoughts, which can then fuel feelings of self-doubt. When you experience emotions like shame or guilt, it's common for your inner critic to become more active and for you to start focusing on your perceived flaws or mistakes. For example, if you're feeling guilty about not meeting a deadline, you might start berating yourself for being lazy or unproductive, which can lead to self-doubt about your abilities.

Similarly, if you're feeling ashamed about a past mistake, you might start ruminating on your shortcomings and feeling like you're not good enough, which can further erode your confidence and self-esteem. Over time, this negative self-talk can become a vicious cycle, as the more you criticize yourself, the worse you feel about yourself, and the more you doubt your abilities.

Comparison

When you experience fear, it can be easy to compare yourself to others and feel like you're not measuring up. You might see someone else who seems to be handling a situation better than you are or who appears more confident or capable and feels like you're not as strong or competent. This can create self-doubt and erode your confidence, especially if you're already feeling anxious or uncertain about a particular situation. For example, if you're feeling scared about a job interview, you might start comparing yourself to other candidates and feel like you're not qualified or experienced. This can lead to self-doubt and a lack of confidence, which can then impact your performance in the interview.

Fear of failure

Bella had always dreamed of getting married and starting a family, but as she got older, she started to feel anxious about the challenges of marriage. She had heard from friends and family members about how difficult it could be to maintain a healthy and happy relationship, and this made her worry about the future. As a result, she started to feel a fear of failure, worried that she wouldn't be able to handle the challenges of marriage and that she might end up alone.

This fear of failure then led to self-doubt, as Bella started to question her own abilities and worth. She began to think that maybe she wasn't cut out for marriage or that she wasn't good enough to find a partner who would love and respect her. This self-doubt then reinforced her fear of failure, as she became even more convinced that she would fail at marriage.

As a result, Bella started to withdraw from dating and relationships, as she didn't want to risk failure or rejection. This only made her anxiety and fear of failure worse, as she felt even more isolated and alone.

Bella is just one example of how left-hemisphere emotions have made it even harder for people to take action in the future as they become increasingly convinced that they will fail. They avoid taking risks or trying new things, which can limit their potential and keep them from achieving their goals.

In conclusion, left-hemisphere emotions can have a significant impact on our lives. While they are normal and unavoidable, it is essential to understand and manage them to prevent them from becoming overwhelming and interfering with our well-being.

Left hemisphere emotions such as resentment, frustration, and anxiety can also lead to self-doubt, making it challenging to pursue our goals and live fulfilling lives. By learning about them, we can learn to manage these emotions and develop resilience, confidence, and a positive outlook on life.

Key Takeaways

- Anger is a normal and natural emotion that arises when we interpret and react to certain situations.

- When you experience negative emotions such as anger or frustration, it's common for your mind to focus on your flaws or mistakes, which can create feelings of inadequacy.

- When you hold onto resentment, you may start to dwell on past events and wish that things could have been different.

- When you are unable to achieve a goal despite putting in the effort, it can lead to feelings of irritability or anger, which are characteristic of frustration.

Chapter 4

The Right Hemisphere Emotions

Happy sensations are only one aspect of positive emotions. Positive emotions such as love, joy, gratitude, contentment, hope, and others help us develop persistent emotional, social, and cognitive assets, which increase our resiliency and mental well-being. They widen our cognitive and cognitive ranges and help us come up with fresh approaches, plans of action, and strategies for dealing with the most challenging circumstances.

Understanding Positive Emotions

Humans are capable of a wide variety of emotions that fluctuate constantly and can persist for a very long time. So how can we describe the good feelings we feel? It is incredibly easy.

Positive emotions are sensations that make us feel good. When it comes to being a person, our genes, experiences, and environment all play a significant role. Therefore, it makes sense that our prior experiences may influence our current emotions. The term "fitness level phenomenon" is frequently used to describe this.

Adaptive-level events occur when we assess our surroundings or circumstances based on prior knowledge. In other words, our happiness level depends on our experiences prior to the present.

The final song they played at your senior prom will always be in your memory. You didn't give that music much thought when you first heard it. Being with all your buddies at that time made you incredibly pleased. But now, each time you hear it, you almost feel the same happiness you did at that particular time.

How we view ourselves concerning others can also impact our emotions. Depending on the individuals around us, we could feel good or bad.

If you think someone is more successful than you, you could feel bad about yourself. But on the other hand, if you think you have more friends, this may make you feel good.

Positive feelings and well-being are inextricably linked; there can be no doubt about that. Positive feelings aid our physical and emotional health. People may heal more rapidly in the hospital if they are filled with optimism and are surrounded by people they love. However, we must first comprehend how unfavourable emotions impact our well-being.

How Positive Emotions Are Formed

Positive emotion-inducing activities abound, and they are all quite effective. Among these, the following are highly effective according to research:

Do Relaxation Techniques

Contentment is the main feeling connected with relaxation techniques. Positive emotions can be reversed, and resilience to negative emotions can be increased via contentment. Meditation, yoga, and muscular relaxation exercises are all examples of relaxation techniques.

The key to increasing the positive meaning in your life is to practice being attentive to it all the time. Use these three methods to uncover a positive meaning in whatever situation you find yourself in. The benefit is that people with many meaningful experiences in their lives will feel more of the whole spectrum of happy feelings.

Just Smile

Because our brains cannot distinguish between a genuine and a false smile, when you fake a smile, your brain reacts by releasing the same "happy chemicals" that it would have otherwise. Therefore, even pretending to feel good might have a real positive effect.

Practice what you love.

Everyone will have diverse and distinctive favourites. Please ensure you know your favourites and that they are constantly accessible. Soccer, reading, and cooking are a few of my favourites. These activities help me unwind, feel good, and temporarily forget about the outside world.

Bounce Back and Move On

Negative emotions may spiral out of control in response to a horrible breakup, losing a loved one, or losing a career. While going through the entire mourning process is advised, it's important to remember that the longer you concentrate on the loss, the longer it will take to recover.

You can start feeling happy by making the decision and trying to move on after a breakup or any other negative experience.

Break Away from Habits That Boost Negative Feelings

What is harming your emotional state? It's usually something over which you have no influence. However, have you ever thought such behaviours might raise your unpleasant emotions by a few notches?

Feelings of melancholy, irritation, tension, and anxiety are among the emotions that habits like getting little sleep, eating junk food, abusing alcohol and caffeine, and having an untidy home are linked to.

Acknowledge That You Can't Always Change Things

Sometimes you can do nothing to stop bad things from happening to good people. Nevertheless, even though you do not influence how others treat you, you have complete control over your response.

It's OK to respond to a challenging circumstance with a positive outlook rather than trying to change it for the sake of others.

Every day, begin and end with affirmations.

Positive affirmations are sentences that support your self-belief, particularly while you are dealing with weaknesses or trying circumstances. These statements can be made aloud, written on sticky notes, or saved on your phone with reminders to repeat each day's beginning and end. This can aid in smothering negative thoughts and self-doubt.

Notably, positive affirmations do not ignore the current circumstances. On the contrary, they emphasize your ability to overcome it and continue forward while acknowledging the reality of the issue.

The phrase "I am strong enough to get over the state that this breakup has left me in" is a nice example.

Concentrate and work through one feeling good at a time.

Working on all your good feelings on a list at once might often leave you feeling overextended. What if you could pick one uplifting feeling and strive to achieve it? You may sense more accomplishment and growth as a result of this.

Say you want to practice being grateful. Every time you experience gratitude, you can list what makes you feel that way and add it.

Then, you can add more and more exercises and activities related to gratitude into your daily routine, such as journaling and using a thankfulness jar or box to keep track of your blessings before moving on to the next uplifting feeling.

Dwell On Happy Memories

The best times to think back on nice things that have happened in the past are when you are feeling so horrible that you are urgently trying to hang onto a good emotion.

According to research from the Department of Psychology at Rutgers University, reflecting on good times might bring back the feelings associated with memorable occasions and enhance your well-being.

Wallow away to remind yourself that there are still positive aspects to your existence, whether special moments with loved ones, fascinating places you've been, or important turning points in your life.

Always take a moment to think before acting.

Did your parents ever tell you to wait 10 seconds before reacting angrily? Advice is still valid. The time you spend counting can mean the difference between exaggerating a dispute and putting out the flames of rage.

For better focus and to help you relax, experts suggest taking a deep breath after each number. Then you have the option of responding or buying yourself more time before bringing up the subject again.

Even around people, you don't like, try to feel good.

Have you ever encountered someone you believed to be hostile, only to be greeted with a smile? I bet it would have been worse if it had been a scowl.

It's unnecessary to make friends with or be extremely kind to individuals you don't like, but a little warmth and friendliness could elicit positive responses from them. You will have saved yourself some unpleasant emotions even if it doesn't.

Keep a positive attitude even when you are with people you dislike.

Have you ever encountered someone you initially thought was antagonistic, only to be greeted with a smile? It would have been terrible if he had been grinning instead.

Even while it's not required to become close friends with or extend a lot of kindness to people you don't like; a little warmth and friendliness could even generate a positive response from them. If it doesn't, you will still have spared yourself some uncomfortable feelings.

Stay Away from Negative Media

According to the British Journal of Psychology, most news stories are negative, and people tend to focus more on negative media coverage, which affects our minds, moods, and happiness.

You can avoid consuming your leisure time with sad and tragic news and instead try to include some uplifting and enjoyable material.

Spend Time with Optimistic Individuals

Positive thinking rubs off on you in the same way that negativity does. Spending time with individuals that exhibit a variety of positive emotions, such as cheer and happiness, will likewise cause positive emotions to spiral higher in you.

This is a signal to stay close to you and with those who bring you joy for longer to ensure the effect is "nearly constant."

Occasionally, look at some motivational sayings.

Happiness magnets, optimism is. Positive thinking will cause you to attract positive things and positive people. - Former gymnast Mary Lou Retton of the United States

This is one example of the many well-known positive statements that can alter your perspective and how you feel and affect your outlook.

Consistently feed your mind with motivational sayings to foster optimistic emotions.

The General Effect of Positive Emotions on Us

Your outlook on life, mental vitality, connections, and potential can all be uniquely revitalized by positivity.

For instance, love, gratitude, and shared optimism can all keep us engaged in what the other person says.

Research supports it. Experiencing happy emotions, both our own and those of others (such as sharing joy), strengthens bonds that result in numerous positive results, such as improved relationship quality, fewer negative effects, and increased subjective well-being.

Positive positivity can enhance psychological and physical well-being by fostering good emotional experiences at appropriate times to handle unpleasant emotions. Positive feelings thus help develop and maintain strong relationships, indirectly promoting well-being. There are also immediate effects.

Such emotional encounters can lessen long-term stress, assisting people in overcoming hardship and developing resilience.

Positive emotions predict a reduction in depressive symptoms and a lowering of perceived stress. In actuality, research demonstrates a link between unfavourable emotions and worse mental health.

It is crucial to remember that the magnitude of such effects does appear to differ among cultures.

Perhaps it is not unexpected that pleasant emotions have a favourable impact on our well-being. Positive feelings encourage us to work toward significant objectives, let us appreciate significant events, and support adolescent behavioural patterns. All of this benefit our well-being, according to the PERMA model of positive psychology (together with engagement, gratifying relationships, meaning, and achievement).

Basic Positive Emotions

Love

Love is important, as we all know, but we may not realize just how much. Love holds the key to enhancing our mental and physical health more than optimism or happiness. Love nurtures the body and mind; the more you feel it, the more you open up and expand. As a result, you become more tenacious, successful, joyful, and healthy.

Intimacy, passion, and commitment define love as feelings and actions. It entails tenderness, proximity, safety, attraction, affection, and trust. Love has different levels of intensity and can evolve. It is linked to pleasant feelings like joy, enthusiasm, fulfilment, and euphoria.

No matter how many different ways we define love in our culture, the body only recognizes one: love is that fleeting feeling of warmth and connection you have with another living being. Since love is the highest kind of positive emotion, it abides by the rules of positive emotions. As a result, it is a momentary experience that comes and goes just as happiness, serenity, or bliss. The good news is that even if it comprises transient experiences, it will accumulate to forge lasting ties because it is a renewable resource that may be "banked" for use at a later time.

Serendipity

'Fortunate happenstance' is one way to define serendipity. In a 'happy' juxtaposition, we feel remarkably satisfied, for example, in the wrong environment.

However, there is hardly any serendipity when you discover a misplaced sock under the couch while seeking the remote control. Instead, it's the realization that, rather than becoming the rock star you always wanted to be, you are happier having settled down with a wife and kids. You set out on the path for many reasons, but somehow it brought you to your desired destination.

Like chance, serendipity can be the realization that you are entirely at peace and serene during a festival. Somehow, you have discovered it in a location that seems to be the antithesis of serenity.

Did you know that lottery players experience happier neurotransmitters just before hearing the results than when they win? What is left to pursue when you have triumphed?

The epiphany you get when you realize you are where you need to be is serendipity. It is essential to locate that location when we least anticipate it because it is rarely where we imagine it will be. In other words, to find that serendipity, we must start looking for contentment more frequently. When that happens, we can stop pursuing pointless objectives and start finding fulfilment in the now.

Forgiveness

It takes more than just saying the words to forgive. Swartz explains whether the other person merits it or not, "it is an active process in which you make a conscious decision to let go of negative feelings." You start to feel sympathy, compassion, and sometimes even affection for the person who injured you as you let go of your anger, resentment, and hatred.

According to studies, some people are just more forgiving by nature. They thus tend to have lower levels of sadness, anxiety, stress, wrath, and aggression and more life satisfaction. On the other hand, those who harbour resentments are more prone to struggle with severe depression, PTSD, and other medical issues. However, that doesn't mean they can't teach themselves to behave more healthfully. According to a study by the non-profit Fetzer Institute, 62 per cent of American adults feel they need greater forgiveness in their personal life.

Hope

Although hope is a subjective sensation that can be difficult to explain, it is difficult to deny hope's importance and its beneficial effects on people's lives.

People frequently talk about how hope helps them stay strong, sticks by them even in their darkest hours, and helps them through situations that appear hopeless.

Hope keeps us motivated to work toward our objectives and devoted to them. Despite the unpredictability of human existence, hope provides people with a cause to keep fighting and believe that their current situation will be better.

Happiness in anticipation is hope. It is enjoying an imagined future in which wonderful things occur and you feel joy or other pleasant feelings. Since optimism is linked to hope, our inclination toward it can improve a bad situation by making us believe that things can only improve.

Desperation and hopelessness are emotions that can be exacerbated by depression in particular. People tend to experience fewer mental health issues when they are hopeful. On the other hand, those who are in despair are more prone to struggle with depression, anxiety, panic attacks, and other issues.

Pride

An individual's independent personal judgment of their own conduct, actions, assets, relationships, affiliations, self, or identity following common societal and cultural ideals results in pride, which is typically a positive emotion or effect.

Even when you are proud of something someone else did, pride is essentially about you. You can also take pride in the accomplishments of people you know and love, such as your kids or your favourite sports team. People can feel pleased with their beauty, family name, or culture without having to actively contribute to the admirable thing1. The best example of how important other people's opinions are is when you deliberately do something that gets people's approval.

Key Takeaways

- Every person has the intrinsic propensity to focus on the bad things that happen to them or those around them.

- To improve our mental, emotional, social, and physical health, despite this, we are capable of developing positive emotions to balance the bad ones.

- The list above provides some tried-and-true suggestions to get you started. There are a variety of techniques to improve or develop pleasant feelings.

- Though most of the advice above should help, it might be time to contact a therapist if you are still having trouble controlling your negative emotions.

- Remember that feelings of happiness are only one component of the puzzle. Be mindful of squelching negative feelings as they arise and swiftly replace them with something more positive because they can seriously hinder any advancement you make with positive emotions.

Chapter 5

The Emotional Capacity of Love

"If we look at the world with a love of life, the world will reveal its beauty to us."

~Daisaku Ikeda

Just like you and me, everyone has both physical and emotional needs. Think of some basic survival needs like water, shelter, food, and air. Having access to these things can make us exist and remain active as humans, but it takes more than all that to give life the actual meaning it deserves. You will agree with me that there are some things you can't touch or see, something like affection, companionship, security, love, happiness, and all. Yet they are incredibly vital in giving our life meaning.

Love, of course, is part of it. It is one of the essentials that we desire as humans to add beauty to our lives and make them more colourful. As humans, we care for physical touch, loving words, sexual intimacy, and kind gestures. But we can't get those things unless we love or we are loved. One thing that happens when we give or receive love is that we are emotionally satisfied. Most especially when the love we give receives equal or higher proportion. Our lives become more meaningful and fulfilling. We also gain the capacity to handle difficult situations because we draw support and strength from our loved ones. The love we receive gives us the power to push through the ups and downs that life is fraught with.

Understanding the Emotional Needs Call Love

Love is a complex word that has no concise definition. But we can say that it has to do with a mix of emotions and behaviours, which are often associated with a strong feeling of affection, respect, and protectiveness toward another person. The word 'I love You' is a common word that we use today, whether we mean it or not. In fact, most people are fond of talking about love even when they know little about it. Love is a common word that both old and young people use when they are emotionally attached to another person.

Love is an emotional need that can exist between family members and spouses, which is most times biologically programmed or culturally indoctrinated. Depending on the cultural milieu, love may vary from person to person. But all in all, it is a feeling that comes with a responsibility – staying committed to helping, respecting, and caring for one another.

One way you can know that you are in love with someone is when you are willing to prioritize the feeling of the person above yours. You just can't say or know why. You always love to put the other person's happiness and wellness first. You just want to stay with the person and promote their opinion above yours without any threat. When we feel this way, it means we are beginning to understand the core of our lives. Do you know why? Love is the core of our lives. It is the purpose, passion, and meaning of life.

Love is an emotion that can be nurtured. In other words, if you discover you don't feel the same way a person feels concerning you. You can allow yourself to flow naturally into loving the person. This doesn't come with force. As in, you don't have to force your way into the person's heart. What you do is to simply make the person know you are worth being in their life through your actions and words.

Love Matters to Life

We may have a ton of relationships, but we all need important people in our lives. People who have seen our flaws and freak flag many times when it comes out and still decided to stick around. People who tag us in captivating memes and tasty videos they know we would love to see. People who text us with random pictures of bumper stickers with hilarious captions.

We all need these close connections to feel a sense of belonging and security in a world that is filled with uncertainty and hatred. We need people who think of us, who look out for us, accept us, and challenge us to bring the best out of us and make us become a better version of yourselves.

This doesn't necessarily mean your spouse or someone you are in a romantic relationship with. It could be the family you were born into, one that you chose, or the one that chose you after pulling down the big wall you erected to keep yourself safe. Anyone that makes everything seem manageable and less stressful for you.

Whether you are having a bad day at work, or a hard struggle to conquer, receiving a call or a hug from the person you share an emotional affinity with can remind you that life is worth a living. It can tell you why love matters in life. And when things are rosy, you have people you can share some pleasurable moments with.

Most of us will agree that love matters to life and that our relationships are essential things to life. The fact is that it is easier to deal with unpleasant circumstances as long as we have people we love who are healthy and safe. You see, it is very easy to lose sight of the bigger picture when we are faced with the struggles of our daily lives. We can even deprioritize the little things that strengthen our relationship when we are worried about our deadlines and debt.

You know, we all have this negativity bias that makes us more sensitive to what's wrong going on instead of focusing on what is right. That's how we are wired, and it's been a means to ensure we are safe.

However, life is beyond being safe. We should get to a stage in our life where we focus more on what we love than what we fear. We want to be proactive, not just reactive, as we always do. We should wake up every day and be the answer to someone's long-time prayers by ensuring we place ourselves in a position where we are a blessing to others.

Why Love is Important to our lives

Whether we accept this fact or not, love rules the world. People make sacrifices to love and put smiles on the faces of others every day because they love. Love is a feeling that comes with a decision to care for another unconditionally, and many people are making it every day to ensure that even the unreached feel some sense of humanity. Below are ways to love our lives better;

Love strengthens and serves as our source of motivation.

The fact that we have people in our lives that care and support us gives us another hope that life is worth living. Love makes us understand that we are not living for ourselves alone but also for others. The truth is that some people love to see us around. Seeing these people around us every day gives us strength that no matter how hard life challenges might be, we are going to thrive. The feeling that we have of people that care for us gives us strength. I can tell that the reason why some people quickly give up on life is that there are no people to show them love. Many people who commit suicide may not have done that if there is someone sticking around and reviving their hope that there are yet more reasons to live than to die.

The fact is, things can never be rosy all the way. There will definitely be some periods when things are hard and almost impossible to forge ahead with, but love will connect us with people that can identify with us in our low estate. In fact, having the feeling of love in the heart alone changes our mindset about life. We begin to have positive thoughts about life, and we will find no reason to envy those who genuinely love.

Love Heals All Emotional Disorders

Quite a number of findings have revealed that one of the reasons why people give up on life is because of mental and psychological disorders we pass through daily. For instance, the feeling of loneliness stimulates anxiety. So, being attached to someone can help put anxiety at bay.

Love Promotes the Right Mindset/Attitude to Life.

Love can make us have a positive perception or view towards something that we could have ordinarily zeroed out. It may be hard to get the best part of life if all we do is focus on the negative side of life. So, what love makes you do is shift your energy to things that are positive so you don't have to worry about negative things that are out of your control.

It brings Comfort and Support.

It is dangerous to pass through life's challenges alone without someone who can offer you a shoulder to lean on whenever you are weary or tired. When we look deeply, we will discover that life is not a one-man thing. You will be in some situations where you need support. An unpleasant situation may occur when you need people to rally around and comfort you. Not having anyone who cares about many makes the emotional wound linger for long.

Love promotes a sense of comfort and support because there is someone somewhere who wants to see you grow and promote your opinions. You may not give them the best, but they are willing to go out of their way to give the solid support you need to scale through the situation you meet yourself.

Love Breaks Barriers

Do you know that true love helps break cultural, ethnic, and religious biases? Yes, one of the powers of love is that it infiltrates into the cultural and ethnoreligious cycle and promotes humanity above others. This is the reason we can talk about inter-religion marriages and affiliation today. We become more tolerant and promote each other's views regardless of our ethical, socio-religious background. Imagine a life without love! We will have to cage our emotional needs and be unable to live life to the fullest as we ought to live. People who are in love learn how each other's culture interprets and expresses love and develop a unique way of showing love.

Being in Love improves our psychological and mental wellbeing

The best way we can improve our mental and psychological well-being is to have more people around us. Being lonely or isolated affects our emotional state, but when we are around our family and friends, our brain stimulates a chemical reaction known as dopamine which makes us happy, calm, and peaceful.

Love forms the basis of our spirituality.

Love is the bedrock of spirituality because we are spiritual beings. One mistake we often make is to equate love with sexuality and affection alone. But we fail to realize that our personal relationship, including romantic ones, strengthens our love life. With love, it becomes easy for us to embrace, tolerate, and forgive people.

It is a way to boost self-confidence.

People who are in healthy relationships or have positive people around them tend to be more confident in all areas of their lives. It has been observed that getting married to the right person or staying around people who care about you helps reduces depression. According to Professor Jacques Snyman, Clinical Advisor for Resolution Health Medical Scheme, "*Having positive self-esteem comes from being validated and receiving affirmation that you have worth. With improved self-esteem, people in love are often more capable of achieving and maintaining their professional and personal goals in life.*"

Why You Should Grow Your Relationships

To build a loving relationship that yields concrete benefits, below are tips you need to implement;

Get treated

If you've had some emotional down moments or have been wounded emotionally, it is important you get treatment. If you are feeling depressed or anxious, seek out the best method to get yourself treated instead of staying calm and untreated. Not treating yourself will definitely affect your love life and relationship with others. Do you know what it is? You deserve the best in life. You are worth the happiness and genuine attraction that relationship brings, and you can't reprieve yourself from the numerous advantages of love because you were wounded. It is time to heal up and start your life afresh. Start from where you left it because there's more to life you have not seen yet. Never let yesterday's affairs determine how your day will be.

Brush up on communication skills and learn to handle conflict.

This is another tip you should do to enhance your love and relationship life. We are quick to tag someone who has been mean or difficult to understand, but somehow, it is because we don't know how to effectively communicate with them. But in actual sense, we need to brush up on communication skills so we can know how to flow with people in our lives.

Do something that excites your loved one on a regular basis.

You can enhance your relationship with people around you by doing things that excite them regularly. When you are committed to doing things that excite people in your cycle, they tend to value and respect you. They will also be more committed because doing so is a sign of commitment to the relationship.

Celebrate each other's successes.

Show that you are lovable and always go after the good of others by celebrating the win, even if it is little others. When you celebrate them, it is a way to show that you value and respect them. It will further show that you are proud of their efforts and achievement and that you can relate and identify with them in their struggle.

In conclusion, love remains a great force that pulls the entire human race together. It helps us place humanity first and bridges the gap that is created due to distrust, hatred, and many more. Love is a natural healer and a remedy to the fractured society we find ourselves in. We all need it to become emotionally satisfied and live a meaningful life.

Key Takeaways

- Love is a forceful and effective tool that pulls the entire human race together.
- No one can live a meaningful life without having people in their cycle who care, respect, and show them a strong feeling of affection.
- Life is worth living if we have people who can support, comfort, and give us strength when we are weak or unable to face the challenges that life throws at us.

Chapter 6

Serendipity

You never know where life will take you, and sometimes the most unexpected moments can lead to the most incredible experiences. Olivia's testimony is live.

Olivia was on a business trip to New York City, feeling tired as she walked down the busy streets. She had just finished a long day of meetings and was looking forward to a quiet night in her hotel room when she saw something that caught her eye. It was a small art gallery tucked away in a side street, and for some reason, Olivia felt drawn to it. She hesitated for a moment, wondering if she had the energy to explore something new, but then decided to take a chance.

As she stepped into the gallery, she was struck by the beauty of the artwork on display. She began to wander around, taking in the colours and textures, and before she knew it, she had struck up a conversation with another visitor - a woman named Lily. Lily was also from out of town and was equally captivated by the artwork. They started chatting about their favourite pieces and soon found themselves talking about their lives, their hopes, and their dreams.

Over the next few days, Olivia and Lily kept running into each other. They went to a concert together, explored the city, and shared late-night conversations over drinks. Before they knew it, they had become the best of friends. But it wasn't until months later that Olivia realized the true power of their serendipitous meeting. As she struggled with a difficult decision in her personal life, she found herself turning to Lily for support and guidance. And as they talked, she realized that the universe had brought them together for a reason - to help each other through the ups and downs of life.

The truth is, we have all been there. We have had moments of serendipity in our lives. Maybe it was something as simple as finding a dollar bill on the street just when you needed it most or meeting someone who became your best friend, just like Olivia, or even your soulmate unexpectedly. Whatever it was, it probably felt like the universe was giving you a little nudge in the right direction.

Serendipity is indeed a fascinating and mysterious emotion or emotion. It seems to be a mixture of chance and fate, luck and intuition, accident and sagacity. It's something that happens when we least expect it but desperately need it. It's a happy accident that changes our life for the better, even though we were not looking for it.

Serendipity is often associated with creativity, innovation, and discovery. It's the spark of inspiration that comes out of nowhere and leads to something amazing. It's the sudden realization that we have been working on the wrong problem all along and that the real solution lies in a different direction. It's an unexpected encounter with someone who shares our passion and vision and who can help us achieve our goals.

Serendipity is also a key ingredient of happiness and well-being. It's the ability to appreciate the small things in life and to find joy in unexpected places. It's the capacity to adapt to change and to see positivity in every situation. It's the courage to take risks and to trust our instincts. It's the belief that everything happens for a reason and that we are always guided by a higher power.

But serendipity is not just a matter of luck or chance. It's a mindset, a way of thinking and living, that opens us up to new possibilities and experiences. It's the willingness to embrace uncertainty and ambiguity and to explore the unknown. It's the curiosity to ask questions and seek answers and the humility to admit that we don't have all the answers.

Difference Between Serendipity And Luck

A lot of people often use serendipity and luck interchangeably, but there is a subtle difference between the two. Luck is generally considered to be a matter of chance - something good happens to us without any rhyme or reason. Serendipity, on the other hand, involves a combination of chance and our own actions or reactions. In other words, serendipity is often the result of being in the right location at the right time and having an open mind and attitude to recognize and take advantage of unexpected opportunities.

For instance, you're walking down the street, and you find a $20 bill lying on the ground. You might consider that a stroke of luck - something good happened to you purely by chance. However, if you happened to be walking down that street because you decided to take a different route to work that day and you happened to look down at just the right moment to see the $20 bill, that could be considered an example of serendipity. In this case, your actions (choosing a different route) and your perceptual awareness (noticing the $20 bill) contributed to the positive outcome rather than it being purely a matter of chance.

Another example might be meeting someone who becomes an important mentor or friend. If you happen to be introduced to that person purely by chance - say, you happen to be standing in the same line at a coffee shop - that could be considered luck. But if you strike up a conversation with that person because you happen to notice a book they're reading that you're also interested in, and that leads to a deeper connection, that could be considered an example of serendipity. In this case, your actions (starting a conversation) and your perceptual awareness (noticing the book) played a role in creating a positive outcome.

So, while luck is often a matter of chance, serendipity involves a combination of chance and our own actions or reactions.

The Effect of Serendipity on Us

Just like every other positive hemisphere emotion, serendipity significantly impacts our lives. In this section, we'll explore the different ways that serendipity can impact our lives. Let's proceed.

Serendipity can bring unexpected joy and happiness into our lives.

Serendipity is a wonderful thing that can add a lot of joy and happiness to our lives. It's that feeling of unexpected good fortune or luck that can come seemingly out of nowhere.

Think about a time when you stumbled upon something amazing by chance - maybe you found a new favourite restaurant while wandering around an unfamiliar neighbourhood, or you met someone who ended up becoming a close friend or even a romantic partner just by striking up a conversation in a random setting. These are the types of experiences that can bring us so much joy and excitement, and they're often the result of serendipity.

The amazing thing about serendipity is that it can remind us to be open to new experiences and to approach the world with a sense of curiosity and wonder. When we're open to the unexpected, we're more likely to stumble upon something truly amazing. And even when things don't turn out exactly as we hoped, the experience of trying something new or stepping outside of our comfort zone can still bring a sense of fulfilment and growth.

It can lead to new opportunities, friendships, and relationships.

Serendipity can often lead us down unexpected paths that open up new opportunities, introduce us to new people, and create meaningful relationships that we might not have otherwise discovered.

For example, let's say you attend a networking event for your job, not really expecting much to come of it. But while you're there, you strike up a conversation with someone who happens to be in your industry and shares your interests. They introduce you to someone else, who introduces you to another person, and before you know it, you've made several valuable connections that could help advance your career.

Or, maybe you're travelling alone in a foreign country, and you accidentally end up on the wrong bus. As a result, you meet a friendly local who speaks your language and offers to show you around their hometown. You spend the day exploring together and end up forming a close bond that lasts long after your trip is over.

These kinds of experiences are valuable, both personally and professionally. They can open up new doors, broaden our perspectives, and help us build connections with others that can greatly benefit our lives in countless ways.

They can also inspire creativity and new ideas

Serendipitous experiences have a way of shaking up our routines and exposing us to new and unexpected ideas, which can lead to increased creativity and fresh perspectives.

For example, imagine you're walking through an art museum and stumbling upon a piece of art that speaks to you in a profound way. That artwork might inspire you to think about your own life or experiences in a new way or to see the world around you with fresh eyes. You might find yourself generating new ideas or insights that you wouldn't have had otherwise.

Similarly, maybe you're stuck on a problem at work or in your personal life, and you can't seem to find a solution. But then, by chance, you overhear someone talking about a completely unrelated topic, and suddenly a new idea or solution pops into your head. That moment of serendipity might be just what you needed to break out of your mental rut and approach the problem from a different angle.

Serendipity can be a powerful force for creativity and innovation, as it exposes us to new experiences and perspectives that we might not have sought out on our own. By staying open to the unexpected and embracing the unknown, we can tap into our own creativity and potentially unlock new ideas and insights that could lead to personal or professional growth.

Serendipity can help us break out of our routines.

Serendipity can be a powerful force in helping us break out of our routines and stay open to new experiences and possibilities.

It's easy to get stuck in our day-to-day routines, doing the same things over and over again and falling into patterns that can feel limiting or even suffocating. But when we experience serendipitous moments, it can help us remember that the world is full of unexpected surprises and opportunities.

For example, maybe you're used to going to the same coffee shop every morning before work. But one day, your usual coffee shop is closed, so you decide to try a different one. While you're there, you strike up a conversation with someone new and end up discovering a shared interest that leads to a new friendship or opportunity.

These experiences can be powerful reminders that life is full of possibilities and that we don't have to be confined to our routines. Serendipity can help us break out of our comfort zones and try new things, which can be a powerful way to grow and learn.

Of course, we can't rely on serendipity alone to help us break out of our routines - we also need to actively seek out new experiences and opportunities. But by staying open to the unexpected and embracing the unknown, we can increase our chances of experiencing those moments of serendipity that remind us of the endless possibilities that exist in the world around us.

How to Attract More Serendipity into Your Life

Serendipity is often associated with chance encounters and unexpected events that lead to positive outcomes. However, while serendipity is often considered a spontaneous stroke of luck, there are ways to attract more of it into your life. In this section, we'll explore some actionable tips on how to create more opportunities for serendipity to occur and bring positive change into your life. Let's proceed.

Know what you want

Knowing what you want is crucial when it comes to attracting more serendipity into your life. It's difficult to stumble upon unexpected opportunities and experiences if you're not even sure what you're looking for. But how do you figure out what you want?

It might seem simple at first - you want a new job, a new city to live in, a new relationship, or a new creative venture. But as you navigate through changes and transitions in your life, you may find yourself feeling uncertain about what you want next. That's why you must take the time to get clear on what truly makes you come alive.

What brings you joy? What makes you feel excited? What activities or pursuits do you lose track of time while doing? Answering these questions can help you identify your passions and interests and can give you a clear idea of what you want to pursue in your life.

By being clear on what you want, you'll be more likely to notice the opportunities and experiences that come your way and to recognize the ones that align with your goals and passions. So, take the time to get clear on what you want, and open yourself up to the serendipitous experiences that may come your way.

Declare your intentions

Once you've gotten clear on what you want, it's important to put it out into the world. Declare your intentions and claim them as if they're already happening. For instance, if you're looking to feel more creatively inspired by starting video blogs, give it a name and list out your intentions for it. Tell yourself every day that this is important to you and that it's already happening. Be excited about it, and let the positive energy you generate by doing so attract more opportunities your way.

Another way to help put your desires out there is to tell people about your plans. Share your aspirations with those who will support you and encourage you in your journey. Not only will this give you a sense of accountability, but it also increases the likelihood that opportunities will come your way through the people you know.

Remember, the more you express your desires, the more likely you are to attract serendipitous experiences that align with your goals and passions.

Act on your intentions

Once you are sure of what you want and have put it out into the world, it's time to take action. You can talk about your desires all you want, but it's only through action that they become a reality. Even if you don't feel fully prepared or qualified, take a leap of faith and just do it. As the saying goes, a dream without action is merely a hallucination. Remember, nobody is an expert in something they've never done before, but every expert was once a beginner. Don't allow your fear to hold you back from pursuing what makes you come alive. You might not get it right on the first try, but through taking action, you'll learn and grow. Clarity comes from action, so take that first step toward your dreams today.

Leave room for it

To attract more serendipity into your life, it's important to leave room for it to happen. After you've taken action toward your goals and aspirations, allow the universe to work its magic. While it's essential to focus and take massive action with clear intentions, it's equally important to let go and trust that things will come together organically.

When you let go and leave room for serendipity, you may find that new opportunities arise, people will enter your life, and you'll start to have conversations about how cool it is that you're attracting exactly what you've been asking for.

Keep in mind that you become what you believe. So be mindful of your thoughts and beliefs and draw positivity into your life. By doing so, you'll be more open to serendipitous moments and experiences that can bring joy, happiness, and new opportunities into your life.

In conclusion, in a world that is increasingly complex and unpredictable, serendipity is more important than ever. It reminds us that life is full of surprises and that the best things often come when we least expect them. It's a source of hope and inspiration and a reason to keep going even when things seem impossible.

So, embrace serendipity in your life. Be open to new experiences and opportunities. Take risks and follow your heart. Believe that things happen for a reason and that you are always guided by a higher power. And who knows? Maybe the next fortunate happenstance is just around the corner, waiting for you to discover it.

Key Takeaways

- Serendipity is a happy accident that changes our life for the better, even though we were not looking for it.

- Serendipity is often associated with chance encounters and unexpected events that lead to positive outcomes.

- Serendipitous experiences have a way of shaking up our routines and exposing us to new and unexpected ideas, which can lead to increased creativity and fresh perspectives.

- To attract more serendipity into your life, it's important to leave room for it to happen.

Chapter 7

Forgiveness

The forgiveness project shares the experiences of those wronged and harmed by others — including parents, friends, family members, and strangers — yet has discovered forgiveness's power. Charlie Ryder, who experienced verbal and physical abuse from his father as a child, is one of those who recounted their experiences. Attacked brutally in his own house was Paul Kohler. A schizophrenic neighbour brutally murdered Anne Marie Hagan's father, and Simon Wilson was the victim of a hit-and-run vehicle accident that left him crippled.

All of these people had trouble forgiving their perpetrators and, in some cases, themselves when they were the ones who had committed the offences. Each had difficulty forgiving since they had gone through various feelings, including wrath, hatred, grief, bitterness, self-pity, want for vengeance, fear, and more. However, thanks to the forgiveness project's intervention, they have realized they must be sorry at various times. And only a select few have reached that particular state of forgiveness-based wholeness.

Individually, we may all identify with experiences of being offended, whether in seemingly insignificant ways, such as when someone cuts in front of us in line, or tragic ones, like when someone physically harmed a loved one or us. Forgiving the perpetrator in these common situations can be very challenging, yet it is possible.

Learning to forgive oneself when we've messed up is frequently easier said than done, especially if we cannot normally resolve conflicts, make reparations, and move on. Fortunately, self-forgiveness can be trained, just like a muscle, and it often becomes much easier to rely on over time. It may be helpful to know what difficulties you might have while you practice self-forgiveness and to seek expert assistance.

Understanding Self-forgiveness

When you forgive someone or yourself, you can accept the acts and behaviours that took place while remaining open to moving forward. Likewise, it does not imply that you are exempt from responsibility for what occurred or that you are OK with what has occurred. You are not weak if you choose to forgive yourself.

Since it might be challenging to go on without closure, many people find it challenging to learn to forgive themselves. It may be necessary to let go of the thoughts and sensations triggered by what went wrong to forgive yourself. Even though it's easy to be our own harshest critic, you should attempt to treat yourself with the same grace that you would anyone else.

The Moment We Err

Learning how to practice self-acceptance and self-forgiveness can be challenging, largely because doing so frequently necessitates acknowledging unpleasant thoughts and feelings. Some see the act as a reminder that they are not flawless. Others view it as a strategy for loving yourself despite your flaws.

Many people desire to move on but struggle to do so without taking the required steps to achieve inner peace. Understanding, sensitivity, and consideration are frequently necessary for self-forgiveness. People might not be aware they can forgive themselves because it takes practice and acceptance that it is a choice. Various aspects of your life may be impacted by how you handle this.

Here are a few reasons for practising self-forgiveness

Forgiveness also springs from our spirituality. Since forgiveness is such a richer-than-life element, it isn't easy to make genuine advancements without it. Fundamentally, it also supports our ego. We must let go if we want to put things right. By continuing to hold on to the past wrongdoings of others or ourselves, we will damage our self-esteem and mar the greatest version of who we may be.

In actuality, there is already enough hatred, suffering, and persecution. Maintaining erect structures on top of what is destructive and harmful is pointless. The best choice you could ever make would be to learn to let go and let yourself radiate love.

You will find peace of mind.

You find calm through forgiving yourself. You begin to focus on crucial things and cease being held hostage by any resentment or grudges you might have. You can let go and demonstrate your readiness to accept freedom. It would help if you were completely let go to fully embrace serenity; there is no such thing as partial letting go.

You show strength

The ability to forgive gives you control over the circumstances, whether it be through fairness or courage. When you are overcome with rage and contempt for your prior transgressions, you cannot truly comprehend this profundity. Only when you are prepared to let go can you accept and comprehend this. It is difficult to forgive or let go because you may feel that doing so demonstrates some weakness or imposes some restrictions. On the other hand, when you can forgive yourself no matter what, everything is different. Feeble cannot pardon. Only the powerful may. Be courageous and forgiving of yourself.

You embrace a gift

Forgiveness is a gift we may give to ourselves, much like the gift of sunshine or rain. All of this results from realizing our spirituality and realizing that we were created to be free from all constraints and live happy lives. We are made to be independent and able to overcome challenges. You can only benefit fully from this gift of forgiveness if you are willing to let go. You must accept this gift and take responsibility for your life.

You show responsibility

Your decisions and subsequent actions are your responsibility. The decision shouldn't be made out of regret, anger, or error.

It would help if you decided on the course of action that is best for you. When you forgive yourself, you assume full responsibility and control of your life and what will happen to you.

Why You Need to Forgive Others

When you forgive someone, you forgive yourself.

Although it may be a cute little catchphrase, that statement is accurate. It's not only about what the other person did to you that makes you want to hold a grudge against them. It has to do with what you have permitted to occur to you. Sometimes, because you're just going along with your routine, you can't control what happens to you in a relationship. You may not always know someone's anger, resentment, or jealousy toward you unless they tell you. And frequently, they wait until a crisis point—often a betrayal—when everything comes to light before they do.

Giving helps you escape victim mode.

The links that tie you negatively to another person are broken by forgiveness. It's possible to forget while also forgiving. What occurs when you experience That cannot be disputed. And it would help if you didn't try to act like everything is fine again. It's not. You might choose to forget about someone once you've forgiven them. After everything is said and done, that is your decision. The question is whether you can ever trust that person or the situation again.

Once you are no longer a victim or under the influence of negative energy, you can concentrate on developing your strength, establishing your own integrity, and developing your own character so that you never again allow yourself to be put in a position of awful compromise and suffering.

Forgiveness frees you

This will enable you to regain control. You now have the opportunity to redirect the energy and emotion you had previously invested in someone or something negative to your growth and emotional, psychological, and physical wellness. You are no longer bound to a force that drains your strength and extinguishes your life. And by liberating yourself, you might be able to view this person or situation in a completely new way. You might be able to remember all the advantages previously there and possibly still if you forgive instead of focusing on all the bad.

Forgiveness helps your health.

Your energy is sapped by negative emotions, which also harm your body, mind, and spirit. Your body is negatively affected by stress, anger, anxiety, and despair. This may increase heart rate, blood pressure, and feeling out of control. The intensity can range widely from minor discomfort to strong physical reactions. Being at odds with someone you care about is, at the absolute least, extremely uncomfortable. Most of us can identify with the relief we get when a burden is removed. We sigh with satisfaction.

Forgiving enables you to move forward on your spiritual path

Compassion is stimulated through forgiveness. You can connect with others because you have had human experience. Just as you feel for yourself, so do other people. You can start to put the past behind you once you are emotionally and psychologically free. An act of goodness and goodwill is forgiveness. It leads to serenity.

How To Practice Self-Forgiveness

Define Forgiveness

The first step is to define forgiveness clearly and understand what it means to you. Your ideologies, family, or religion could influence your definition. Please make sure you are clear about what forgiveness is not before you describe it. It will feel like you are absolving yourself of responsibility if you think that forgiveness absolves you of blame or indicates that you are not to blame.

You'll be trapped in guilt or denial if you think of forgiving as forgetting or moving on as if nothing occurred. Because of this, it's critical to establish a precise definition of forgiveness. Maybe the definition of forgiveness is the choice to accept that you are flawed and have made bad decisions that have hurt others. However, you are choosing to treat yourself with compassion and understanding rather than continue to punish yourself and wallow in self-pity. By doing this, you will be able to learn from this experience, take responsibility for your choices, and develop in ways that will support lasting transformation.

Acknowledge Your Feelings

You need to accept your sentiments rather than suppress them to forgive yourself. Make time to think about your sentiments without passing judgment. Identify your feelings and permit yourself to feel them. You are free to feel whatever you need, and those sentiments don't have to determine your reactions. Even though it might be challenging, you must identify, experience, and permit yourself to work through guilt and shame before you can let them go. Remorse is a common emotion to have after hurting another person. Acknowledging these emotions helps you comprehend what happened more fully. Ignoring your feelings might increase your remorse, which can make it very challenging to forgive yourself.

Acknowledge What You Did

Without owning up to your mistakes, you can't genuinely learn from them. You can understand why something occurred by accepting responsibility for your part in it and acknowledging what happened. Set your judgment aside and consider what truly happened and your part in the incident. You can take action to prevent doing it again after learning the lessons from what you did. Living in denial prevents you from accepting responsibility for your errors and growing from them.

Repeating the occurrence also prevents you from focusing on what you learned and instead keeps you from focusing on what went wrong. You can take the measures required to implement meaningful adjustments if you can identify the actions and behaviours contributing to the issue.

Apologize

Apologize if your actions hurt someone else. A genuine apology to the person you have offended might go a long way toward helping you forgive yourself. If you still need to make amends with someone else, genuinely forgiving yourself will undoubtedly be difficult. Although you can't predict how the other person will react, apologizing to the offended party can help you move on more quickly and find forgiveness for yourself. If you have wounded someone else but cannot apologize to them, writing down your thoughts can help you avoid dwelling on the incident.

You can also apologize to yourself in writing. If you want to appear sincere in your apology, you must own your mistake, explain why you regret it, express regret for the suffering you have caused, and say what you will change going forward to ensure it won't happen again.

Focus On What You Learned

When something goes wrong, essential lessons are far simpler to learn than when it goes right. You might discover that self-forgiveness is more appropriate if you can concentrate on the learning experience and what you will do better in the future. You can choose differently in the future once you are aware of what you did and the results. Sometimes making a mistake is the best way to learn this lesson. It is common to fixate on your mistakes, but you might not learn too much if that is all you think about. You can learn from the event by concentrating on the changes you should make.

You might be able to start extending forgiveness to yourself once you see it as a difficult lesson.

Make Meaningful Changes

The first step is recognizing that your actions created a problem. You might need to adjust your behaviour to forgive yourself. It would help if you also altered your conduct. You are not accepting responsibility for what you did if you keep engaging in the troublesome activity. Only by altering behaviour is it possible to achieve better results. For instance, if you consistently arrive late for work and feel horrible about it, you can modify this by setting an earlier departure time from home.

If changing your behaviour won't make a difference, you can still have a significant effect in another way. You may help out by volunteering, telling people your tale, or coming up with a future solution. Paying it forward is a smart technique to change your perspective from what you did wrong to what you are doing about it.

Practice Compassion

You can have compassion for yourself in the same way that you have compassion for others. Beating yourself up about something you can't undo after it's happened only reinforces the negativity. This may cause you to think that you are a broken person unworthy of grace. Instead, you can be kind to and accepting of yourself. Speak to yourself like you would your closest friend. Recognize that you are not a mistake just because you made a mistake. The way you treat yourself is a decision, even though you are probably harsher on yourself than you are on anyone else. You can learn to forgive others and yourself by treating yourself with kindness and understanding. Although it may not be simple, your emotional well-being must forgive yourself. Individual counselling may help if you have trouble forgiving yourself for past transgressions. Keep in mind that you can forgive yourself without having to forget what happened. You can undergo significant growth and transformation to enhance your general well-being when you forgive yourself.

The Power of Self-forgiveness

Self-forgiveness is a crucial step linked to mental wellness. However, there is a big difference between taking responsibility for your words and deeds and placing the blame on yourself.

Beating yourself up for what you said or did is not a part of accepting responsibility for your ideas, feelings, and behaviours. You can forgive yourself and make better decisions in the future by acknowledging your shortcomings and appreciating the shared humanity.

Self-forgiveness is learning to distinguish between guilt and shame and overcoming your shame. It also entails accepting those aspects of yourself that you once found undesirable.

Everybody has self-critical thoughts when they make a mistake. On the other hand, healthy self-criticism can develop into self-blame if you let it get out of control, which is bad for your well-being.

You can accept accountability for your actions and words when you forgive yourself. It prevents you from considering yourself a victim or an offender.

You will reclaim your confidence and begin to believe in yourself once you let go of the idea that you are a bad person.

You will feel more able to consciously notice your thoughts and emotions of anger, hurt, depression, shame, guilt, and self-blame, acknowledge these emotions, and then let them go with the aid of self-compassion.

You will learn to recognize unhelpful ideas and feelings and exchange them for empathy, compassion, and love for yourself through the practice of self-forgiveness.

Self-forgiveness is a tool to take on a new task. It is a means of giving yourself another chance to do better than before. When you forgive yourself, you can challenge yourself by taking on a new role or task.

Key Takeaways

- Your emotional well-being can benefit from self-forgiveness.

- Self-help techniques, online therapy and counselling, are two ways you might work on forgiving yourself.

- Self-forgiveness can require time and work to develop, but the practical tips highlighted in this chapter are constructive ways to learn to let go of the past and focus on the present.

- Acknowledging that you didn't know, didn't comprehend, or didn't behave in a way that could have ended the issue is forgiving oneself.

- By forgiving yourself, you make room for healing to replace hurt and bitterness. You are acting in a way that will correct the course of your life and general well-being.

Chapter 8

Hope

Can you remember how often you have said you are hopeful about a situation? We all claim to be hopeful, but just a few of us truly know what it means. The truth is hope is a powerful emotion that can provide us with the strength and motivation to face difficult times. It arises when we wish for something positive to happen in the future, even if the outcome is uncertain and out of our control. For instance, we might hope for good weather for an outdoor event, wish for our child to pass an exam, or hope for our preferred candidate to win an election.

Hope can also be altruistic, meaning we can hope for positive outcomes for complete strangers or those in distant places. For example, we might hope for peace in a war-torn country or for a cure for a disease.

To experience hope, we need to believe that there is at least a slim chance that the desired outcome can happen. However, if the possibility of it happening is highly likely, we are more likely to experience excitement rather than hope. Additionally, hope is typically felt when we have little to no control over the situation or external factors, like the weather or election outcomes.

The concept of hope is broad, but I would love us to explore it because it's going to be beneficial in living a fulfilling life. Basically, hope has two types of hope: active hope and passive hope. Let's take a closer look at them.

Active hope

Active hope is all about taking charge of your situation and doing everything you can to make your desired future a reality. It's about being proactive and motivated to take action, even when the outcome is uncertain. Active hope is most effective when you have some control over the situation, and it motivates you to make changes that will increase the likelihood of a positive outcome.

Passive hope

On the other hand, passive hope can be problematic when it leads to inaction and waiting for external factors to bring about what we hope for. It can induce passivity, even when we have some agency in the situation. When we wallow in passive hope, we don't recognize that we can make changes and take action to bring about the desired outcome. However, passive hope can be functional in situations where we have little or no control over the outcome. It fosters patience and optimism that better times are coming and encourages us to wait for a more opportune time.

For a better understanding, look at this scenario.

Imagine you're a student who is hoping to get an A on your upcoming exam. You have two options: you can either passively hope that you get a good grade, or you can actively hope and take action to increase your chances of success.

Passive hope might involve wishing for a good grade and doing nothing to prepare for the exam. You might say to yourself, "I hope I do well on this exam," and then spend your time doing other things, like watching TV or playing video games.

On the other hand, active hope involves taking charge of the situation and doing everything you can to make your desired future a reality. So, you might actively hope for a good grade by setting aside time to study, reviewing your notes, and seeking help from your teacher or classmates if needed. You might even take practice exams to assess your knowledge and know areas where you need to improve.

When it comes time for the exam, a person with passive hope might feel anxious and worried, while a person with active hope will feel more confident and prepared. Even if both students end up getting the same grade, the person with active hope will feel more satisfied because they put in the effort to increase their chances of success.

Components of hope

Just like every other type of right hemisphere emotion, there are some components that make up hope. Without them, hope will not be hope. Having an understanding of what they are will help you know what to do when you are being hopeful. Let's proceed.

Goals

The first component of hope is, having a goal. Goals can be big or small, short-term or long-term, but they are the foundation of hope. Goals give you a sense of direction and purpose, something to strive for and work towards.

Think of a goal as a destination on a map. Without a destination, you're just wandering aimlessly. But with a destination, you can plan your route, take detours when necessary, and stay focused on reaching your destination.

Your goal can be anything that you want to achieve, whether it's a personal or professional goal. It could be something as simple as learning a new skill or something as ambitious as starting your own business. The important thing is that it is something that you truly want and believe it is possible to achieve.

Having a goal also means that you have something to measure your progress against. You can track your progress, celebrate your successes, and adjust your plans if necessary. And when you finally achieve your goal, you feel accomplished, which in turn fuels your hope for future goals.

Willpower

Willpower is a crucial component of hope. It's the force that pushes you toward your goal, and it involves the belief that your actions can lead to positive outcomes. When you have willpower, you feel empowered to take action and make choices that align with your goals.

Willpower is not just about having a positive attitude or mindset. It also requires effort, determination, and resilience in the face of setbacks and obstacles. For example, if you're working towards a goal of getting in shape, the agency is what motivates you to get up early for a morning run or to resist the temptation of unhealthy snacks. It's the inner voice that tells you that your efforts will be worth it in the long run and that you have the ability to overcome challenges along the way.

People with high willpower tend to be more optimistic, confident, and proactive in pursuing their goals. They believe in their ability to create positive change in their lives and are willing to put in the necessary work to make it happen. In contrast, people with low willpower may feel helpless, resigned, or stuck in their current situation.

Pathways

Pathways refer to the specific steps or plans you create to achieve your goals. It's like a roadmap that guides you toward your destination. But it's not always a straight and easy path. Sometimes, you might encounter obstacles or challenges along the way that could prevent you from reaching your goal.

This is where high-hope people shine. They understand that setbacks are inevitable and that there might be roadblocks that could derail their progress. However, instead of giving up, they problem-solve to find a new pathway. They are resilient and adaptable, and they can adjust their plans to overcome any hurdles that come their way.

Think of it this way: if your goal is to climb a mountain, there might be multiple routes to reach the summit. You might try one path, but it might be too steep or too dangerous. Instead of giving up, you might look for an alternate route that is safer or more manageable. You might need to take a longer path or make some detours, but as long as you keep your goal in sight and remain determined, you can reach the summit eventually.

High-hope people also understand that failure is not the end of the road. If a pathway doesn't work out, they don't give up on their goal altogether. They reassess and try a new approach. They believe that there is always a way to achieve their aims, and they don't let setbacks discourage them.

Features of hope

As I said earlier, hope is a broad subject that we need to explore. This section will give you a deeper insight into some characteristics of hope.

Scope

Hope can be a powerful force in our lives, and it can serve different functions depending on the situation. Sometimes, we hope for personal goals, like getting a degree or finding love. Other times, we might hope for something that affects people close to us, like our sister finding a new house or our son finishing college. And sometimes, our hopes can be much broader, like hoping for our country to get a new leader or for our favourite sports team to become the champion.

Our hopes can be very specific, like hoping for good weather on our birthday tomorrow, or they can be more abstract and without a clear timeline, like hoping for better times in the future. No matter the object of our hope, it can give us a sense of direction and motivate us to take action toward achieving our desired outcome.

Intensity

Hope is a fascinating emotion that can vary in intensity depending on how much we care about the outcome we're hoping for. When we're hoping for something that is highly relevant to our personal lives, such as finding love or achieving a long-term goal, our hope can be incredibly strong. This is especially true for optimistic people who tend to experience hope more easily.

Interestingly, the less likely an event is to happen, the higher our levels of hope can be. This may seem counterintuitive, but to be honest, it makes sense when you think about it. If something is very likely to happen, we'll likely feel excitement instead of hope. But if it's a long shot, we'll hope for it even more passionately.

That being said, if the likelihood of something happening is too small, we might lose all hope and even become desperate. This is why it's important to strike a balance between realistic expectations and hopefulness. It's okay to daydream and fantasize about the things we hope for, but we also need to believe that there's at least some possibility of them coming true.

Hope is typically a milder emotion that can last for months and sometimes even up to a year. It's often described as a background emotion, meaning that it's not always at the forefront of our minds, but it's always there, quietly nudging us toward our goals. People often use daydreaming and fantasizing as a way to keep hope alive, but it's important to remember that hope is not just wishful thinking.

If we're hoping for something that is largely under our control, such as achieving a personal goal, we might experience determination instead of hope. This is because we believe that our actions can directly impact the outcome we're hoping for.

Copy mechanism

Hope can be a powerful coping mechanism during difficult times. It helps you to shift your focus towards something positive, even in situations where everything seems bleak and negative. By maintaining a sense of hope, you can motivate yourself to "see the bright side" of things and identify opportunities that may have gone unnoticed otherwise. This can give you a much-needed boost in confidence, courage, and ambition, allowing you to not just survive but thrive in challenging circumstances.

In fact, research suggests that hope is essential for both physical and mental well-being. Hopeful people are more likely to recover quickly from illnesses and injuries, and they tend to have a more positive outlook on life. On the other hand, when someone loses all hope, they may no longer see a reason to live.

Regardless of the challenges we may face in life, hope is a resilient emotion that can endure even in the most trying of circumstances. As the saying goes, "Hope dies last," reminding us that even in the darkest moments, we can hold onto the belief that things will get better.

Tips For Becoming More Hopeful

If you're looking to cultivate more hope in your life, there are several things you can do to help you develop a more optimistic outlook. By making some simple changes in your thoughts and behaviours, you can start to feel more positive and motivated about your future. Let's explore some tips for becoming more hopeful.

Think of your goals as exciting challenges

One simple trick to be more hopeful is to start thinking of your goals as exciting challenges. Instead of feeling overwhelmed or anxious about them, try to approach them with enthusiasm and curiosity. Imagine how you'll feel when you finally achieve them. Visualize the details of your success and feel the rush of joy and pride that comes with it.

This simple shift in perspective can make a huge difference in how you approach your goals. By framing them as exciting challenges, you're more likely to stay motivated, take risks, and persevere even when things get tough. So, go ahead and dream big! Embrace the challenges ahead with open arms and let the excitement of what's possible fuel your hope.

Be Flexible and creative

Being flexible and creative is a great way to increase your hopes and increase your chances of success. When you're working towards a goal, it's important to have a Plan A, but it's equally important to have backup plans in case things don't go as expected. This is where plans B, C, D, and so on come in handy.

By developing multiple plans, you're being proactive and preparing for the unexpected. This can help you stay motivated and hopeful even if obstacles arise. Plus, it's an opportunity to get creative and brainstorm new solutions that you may not have considered before.

So, if you're feeling stuck or discouraged, take a step back and consider all of your options. Think outside the box, and don't be afraid to try something new. With a flexible and creative mindset, anything is possible.

Expect setbacks

Kindly keep in mind that achieving something worthwhile is rarely a smooth and easy journey. Along the way, you're bound to encounter obstacles and challenges that may test your resolve. But don't let this discourage you! Instead, anticipate roadblocks and prepare yourself mentally for them.

Knowing that difficulties are likely to arise, you can approach your goals with a more flexible and adaptable mindset. Be open to exploring different approaches and be willing to pivot if your original plan hits a dead end. Remember, sometimes, the road less travelled can lead to even greater success than the beaten path.

Take it one step at a time

Taking it one step at a time is a great way to build momentum and move forward toward your goals. Sometimes, when we set big goals for ourselves, it can feel overwhelming and daunting. But if you break it down into more manageable steps, it becomes much more achievable.

So, if you're struggling to make progress toward your goals, try focusing on just one small step you can take each day. It could be something as small as making a phone call or sending an email, but each small step brings you one step closer to your goal.

By taking it one step at a time, you also give yourself the opportunity to celebrate small victories along the way. Celebrating these small wins can be incredibly motivating and help you stay focused on your ultimate goal.

Be realistic

Setting high but realistic goals is an important aspect of being more hopeful. It's important to aim high but, at the same time, ensure that the goals are attainable. False hope, or hope that is unrealistic or unattainable, can lead to disappointment and a loss of motivation.

By setting high but realistic goals, you're allowing yourself to see the potential for success while also being aware of the challenges that may arise along the way. This kind of positive outlook can inspire you to take steps toward your goals and keep you focused on the end outcome.

Watch your association

Being around others who inspire and uplift us can help us feel more hopeful and motivated. There are many materials, such as books, podcasts, and even social media accounts, that feature stories of people who have overcome significant challenges and achieved great things.

Listening to their stories can help us gain perspective and realize that we, too, can overcome obstacles and achieve our goals. It can also help us feel less alone in our struggles, knowing that others have faced similar challenges and have come out stronger on the other side.

It's best to surround ourselves with positivity and inspiration, especially during times when we may feel discouraged or hopeless.

In conclusion, hope is a fundamental aspect of our lives that can help us face even the most difficult and uncertain times. Whether we're hoping for a personal goal or a global outcome, hope gives us the strength, motivation, and resilience to persevere. By focusing on our goals, being flexible, expecting roadblocks, taking it one step at a time, keeping our goals high but realistic, and gaining strength from others, we can cultivate and nurture our hope. Remember, hope is not a luxury but a necessity for our well-being and flourishing. Let's embrace hope and never lose sight of the possibilities and opportunities that lie ahead.

Key Takeaways

- Active hope is all about taking charge of your situation and doing everything you can to make your desired future a reality
- Passive hope can be problematic when it leads to inaction and waiting for external factors to bring about what we hope for.

- Hope is made up of Goals, Willpower, and Pathways.

- Hope helps you to shift your focus towards something positive, even in situations where everything seems bleak and negative.

- One simple trick to be more hopeful is to start thinking of your goals as exciting challenges.

Chapter 9

Pride

How do you feel when someone tells you that they are proud of you? You feel fulfilled, right? But have you ever told yourself that you're proud of yourself? Regardless of what your answer is, a lot of people don't know what pride is about. In fact, some think that pride is a bad thing and it's not morally right to be proud. But let me burst your bubble; pride is a beautiful thing. Don't be confused; I will explain what pride is.

At its core, pride is a feeling of satisfaction that comes from achieving something praiseworthy or possessing qualities that are highly valued by others. It's that warm feeling you get when you've accomplished something that you've worked hard for and others recognize and appreciate your efforts.

But what makes pride so interesting is that it's not just about the accomplishment itself. It's also about the sense of self-worth and validation that comes from knowing that others see you as someone who is worthy of praise. It's like a little ego boost that makes you feel confident and energized.

And the great thing about pride is that it can come from various sources. Maybe you're proud of your child's achievements, or of your heritage, or of your physical appearance. In each case, the thing that you're proud of becomes a part of your identity and helps to shape how you see yourself in the world.

But here's the thing: even though pride is often associated with individual achievement, it's also deeply connected to our social nature as human beings. That's why it's so important to us what other people think. We want our peers to celebrate and respect us, and we want to feel like we're part of a community that values the same things that we do.

So, in a way, pride is a kind of social glue that helps to bind us together as a society. It allows us to share in each other's successes and to feel connected to something greater than ourselves. And that, in turn, can inspire us to strive for even greater achievements and to be our best selves.

To feel proud, you need some kind of external confirmation that what you're proud of is truly praiseworthy. This can come from other people's opinions or even from your own internalized sense of what is valuable and admirable.

However, this means that other people can also influence whether or not you feel proud. If you're surrounded by people who don't value the things, you're proud of, it can be difficult to feel that sense of validation and self-worth that comes with pride. For example, if you come from a family that values academics, but your peers at school value athleticism, it can be hard to feel proud of your academic achievements if they aren't being recognized and appreciated by the people around you.

Moreover, what is considered praiseworthy is often subjective and relative. It depends on the cultural context and the people you're comparing yourself to. For example, if you're a good runner in a school with average athletes, you might feel incredibly proud of your time. But if you move to a school with highly competitive athletes, those same times might suddenly seem unremarkable.

This is why the exclusivity of your qualities in your surroundings plays a big role in how proud you feel. The rarer and more exceptional your qualities are in your environment, the more praiseworthy they seem and the prouder you'll feel as a result.

All of this goes to show that pride is a complex and deeply social emotion. It's not just about your own individual accomplishments but also about how those accomplishments are valued by the people around you. And as a result, it can be a tricky emotion to navigate as you try to balance your own sense of self-worth with the expectations and opinions of others.

Types of pride

Remember, I said earlier that some people think pride is a bad thing. And that's because they don't know that pride can be a positive emotion. Those people might have only experienced the negative type of pride. This section will detail the two types of pride humans can exhibit. Let's proceed.

Authentic pride

Authentic pride is a powerful emotion that arises when we feel genuinely good about something we've accomplished. It's the feeling of satisfaction and fulfillment that comes from knowing you've done something meaningful and valuable and that you've put in the effort and hard work required to achieve it.

What's interesting about authentic pride is that it's not just about the outcome of what you've accomplished - it's also about the process of getting there. When you experience authentic pride, it's not just because you've succeeded but because you've put in the effort, persevered through challenges, and stayed true to your values along the way.

Authentic pride is a deeply fulfilling emotion because it's a reflection of our own sense of self-worth and personal growth. It's not dependent on the approval or validation of others - although it can certainly be reinforced by positive feedback from others - but rather, it's about feeling good about ourselves and our own accomplishments.

One of the great things about authentic pride is that it can be cultivated and developed over time. By setting meaningful goals, working hard to achieve them, and staying true to your values and principles, you can experience authentic pride more often and more deeply. And as you do, you'll start to feel a greater sense of confidence, self-esteem, and overall well-being.

Hubristic pride

Hubristic pride is a form of pride that is rooted in an inflated sense of self-importance and superiority over others. It's the feeling of being "better than" or "above" others, and it often involves a desire to dominate or control those around you.

Unlike authentic pride, which is based on genuine accomplishments and a sense of personal growth, hubristic pride is often based on external factors such as wealth, status, or power. It's a type of pride that is dependent on the approval and validation of others, and it can lead to a sense of entitlement and arrogance.

The problem with hubristic pride is that it can be destructive to our lives and our relationships with others. When we are motivated by hubristic pride, we may become engrossed with winning at any cost, even if it is by harming others or compromising our own principles. We may also become defensive and resistant to feedback or criticism, which can lead to a lack of self-awareness and an inability to grow and learn.

While hubristic pride may provide a temporary boost to our ego, it ultimately leaves us feeling empty and unfulfilled. It can lead to a sense of loneliness and isolation as we become more focused on our own needs and desires and less attuned to the needs and feelings of those around us.

Benefit of pride

Yes, pride can be beneficial. So, take some time to look at what you gain when you exhibit pride.

Lead to quality output

When you feel proud of what you're doing, you're more likely to set higher standards for yourself and pursue excellence in everything you do.

Think about it: if you take pride in your work, you're not going to settle for mediocrity or half-hearted efforts. You'll want to produce something that truly reflects your skills and abilities and that you can be proud of.

When you set high standards for yourself, you're also more likely to be detail-oriented and thorough in your work. Pay attention to the little things that can make a big difference, and you'll be willing to go the extra mile to ensure that everything is just right.

It means you care

When you care about something, whether it's your work, a hobby, or a relationship, you're more likely to take it seriously and put in the effort needed to succeed.

On the other hand, if you don't take pride in what you're doing, it's often a sign that you don't really care about it. You might be going through the motions, doing the bare minimum, but not putting in the extra effort needed to truly excel.

When you care about something, you're more likely to take ownership of it and feel a sense of responsibility for its success. You'll be invested in the outcome and willing to put in the time and effort needed to ensure that everything turns out the way you want it to.

Taking pride in what you do is also a reflection of your personal values and beliefs. It shows that you have a strong work ethic, a desire for excellence, and a commitment to doing things the right way.

Ultimately, when you take pride in what you do, you're sending a message to yourself and others that you care about the work you're doing and the impact it has on your life and that of the people around you.

Spurs leadership

When you have a strong sense of pride in something, whether it's your work, your community, or your organization, you are more likely to take on a leadership role to protect it. This is because you care deeply about its success and are willing to fight for it.

Pride can give you the confidence to speak up, take charge, and make decisions that will benefit everyone involved. It can also inspire others to follow your lead and work towards a common goal. In this way, pride can be a powerful force for positive change and progress. So, don't be afraid to take pride in what you do and use it to become a leader in your field or community.

How To Use Pride To Your Advantage

It is not enough to learn about pride; you should also know how to use it to your advantage. This section will teach you that. Let's dive in.

Choose your company wisely

Surrounding yourself with the right people can be a great way to use pride to your advantage. People who provide honest feedback, support, and encouragement can help you build a healthy sense of self and can guide you toward reaching your goals. However, it's important to be conscious of the company you keep. Spending time with people who constantly praise you, even when you haven't done anything praiseworthy, can lead to over-inflating your ego and a false sense of pride.

The right kind of people are the ones who will offer genuine appreciation and constructive criticism when necessary. They will help you identify your strengths and weaknesses and push you to become the best version of yourself. Being around such individuals can also help you to learn from their successes and failures, which can further enhance your pride and motivation to succeed. So, choose your company wisely and surround yourself with people who will challenge and support you.

Humility is Key

Staying humble is an important aspect of using pride to your advantage. It means acknowledging your accomplishments without feeling the need to constantly seek praise or attention from others. It's about recognizing that your successes do not define your entire identity.

Humility is also an essential trait for building and maintaining strong relationships with others. It shows that you are open to feedback and willing to learn from your mistakes. Additionally, staying humble can help you avoid the pitfalls of hubristic pride, which can lead to negative consequences such as arrogance and overconfidence.

To stay humble, it's important to recognize that everyone has room for growth and improvement. Instead of focusing solely on your own achievements, take the time to acknowledge and appreciate the accomplishments of others. This can help you develop a more balanced perspective and avoid becoming overly self-centered.

Remember, being proud of yourself is a positive thing, but it's important to maintain a healthy balance between confidence and humility. By staying humble, you can use your sense of pride to motivate and inspire you to continue doing your best work without letting it get in the way of your relationships and personal growth.

Try something new

Trying new things is a great way to use pride to your advantage. It's easy to get stuck in our comfort zones and only do things that we're already good at. However, trying new things can help us expand our horizons and grow as individuals.

When you try something new, you allow yourself to take risks and make mistakes, which can be scary but ultimately rewarding. It's important to remember that it's okay not to be great at something right away. Being a beginner means that there's room for improvement, and every time you practice, you're getting closer to mastering that skill.

Whether it's learning a new language, taking up a new hobby, or trying out a new sport, there's always something new to try. By challenging yourself in this way, you'll not only experience the pride of learning something new, but you'll also develop a growth mindset in all aspects of your life.

Do what you love

Doing what you love can be a great way to tap into your sense of pride without needing external validation. When you're passionate about something, you're more likely to take pride in your work and derive satisfaction from it. It can also help you to be motivated and engaged, even when things get tough. Of course, not everyone has the opportunity of doing work that they love, but even small changes can make a big difference. Maybe you can find a way to incorporate your passions into your work or find a hobby or side project that brings you joy and fulfillment. By focusing on what you love and finding ways to integrate it into your life, you can cultivate a healthy sense of pride that comes from within rather than relying on external sources of validation.

In conclusion, pride is a complex emotion that can both be positive and negative. When we experience authentic pride, we can hold ourselves to high standards, feel a sense of accomplishment, and become leaders who fight for what we believe in. On the other hand, hubristic pride can lead to arrogance, selfishness, and a disregard for others. By surrounding ourselves with positive influences, staying humble, trying new things, and doing what we love, we can use pride to our advantage and achieve a healthy sense of self.

Key Takeaways

- Pride is a feeling of satisfaction that comes from achieving something praiseworthy or possessing qualities that are highly valued by others.

- Authentic pride is a powerful emotion that arises when we feel genuinely good about something we've accomplished.

- Hubristic pride is a form of pride that is rooted in an inflated sense of self-importance and superiority over others.

- Surrounding yourself with the right people can be a great way to use pride to your advantage.

Chapter 10

Validating Your Feelings

In the previous chapters, we have discussed different types of emotions and how they impact our lives. We have learned how positive emotions can enhance our well-being, boost our confidence, and make us feel good about ourselves.

Now, it's time to take things a step further. It's time to talk about validating those feelings and how to do it effectively. By validating our emotions, we are not only acknowledging them but also showing ourselves that we matter and that our emotions are important.

So, whether you're feeling excited, grateful, proud, or any other positive emotion, it's important to validate yourself. Let's dive in and learn how to validate your feelings.

What Does Validation Mean?

Validation is a basic human need. It helps us feel accepted, understood, and valued. When someone tells us they appreciate us, that we've done a good job, or that our feelings are valid, we feel seen and heard. It's a beautiful feeling, isn't it?

Unfortunately, we can't always rely on others to validate us. We can't control how others respond to us; sometimes, people may be dismissive or unsupportive. That's why it's crucial to learn how to validate ourselves.

When we rely on external validation to determine our worth, it can be detrimental to our mental health. We may become anxious or depressed, constantly seeking approval and doubting our abilities if we don't receive it. We may obsessively check our social media posts, hoping for likes and comments that affirm our worth.

But the truth is, relying on external validation is a slippery slope. It can leave us feeling empty and unfulfilled. We become needy and clingy, and this can push others away. That's why it's essential to cultivate self-validation.

Self-validation means acknowledging our thoughts, feelings, and judgments. It means recognizing our worth and trusting our abilities. It's about learning to appreciate ourselves, even when others don't.

When we practice self-validation, we become more resilient. We're less likely to be swayed by other people's opinions and less likely to be affected by criticism or disapproval. We know our worth and don't need anyone else to tell us how amazing we are.

Of course, this doesn't mean that external validation is unimportant. We all want to feel appreciated by others, and there's nothing wrong with that. But external validation should be a supplement to self-validation, not a replacement. In that case, here are some ways to validate your feelings.

Encourage yourself

Encouraging yourself is a powerful way to validate your feelings. It means being your cheerleader and giving yourself the support and motivation to keep going.

When we encourage ourselves, we acknowledge the effort we're putting in and the progress we're making. We remind ourselves of our strengths and why we're pursuing our goals. We also provide positive self-talk, which can help boost our confidence and self-esteem.

Encouraging ourselves can take many forms. For example, we might give ourselves a pep talk before a challenging task or remind ourselves of past successes when we feel discouraged. We might also celebrate our accomplishments, no matter how small they seem.

It's important to note that encouraging ourselves doesn't mean ignoring our challenges or shortcomings. Rather, it means approaching those challenges with a positive mindset and focusing on our progress. We can acknowledge what we need to work on while also recognizing what we are doing well.

Prioritize your needs

prioritizing your needs is another important aspect of validating your feelings. It means recognizing your needs and ensuring they're being met rather than constantly putting other people's needs before yours.

Many of us are taught to prioritize the needs of others above our own, and while it's important to be kind and considerate to those around us, it's equally important to take care of ourselves. When we prioritize our own needs, we're sending ourselves the message that we're valuable and worthy of care.

Prioritizing your needs can take many forms. It might mean setting boundaries with others when you need time for yourself or taking breaks when you feel overwhelmed. It might also mean engaging in activities that make you, even if they don't always align with other people's expectations.

Accepting your flaws

This means acknowledging that you're not perfect and that it's okay to make mistakes or have limitations.

Many of us hold ourselves to impossibly high standards, and when we inevitably fall short, we can be extremely hard on ourselves. But this kind of self-criticism can be harmful and counterproductive.

Accepting your limitations, flaws, and mistakes means recognizing that you're human and that everyone makes mistakes. It means reframing mistakes and failures as opportunities for growth and learning rather than as evidence of your inadequacy.

Speak positive words

Have you ever been stuck in negative self-talk, where you're constantly putting yourself down and feeling like you're not good enough? It's a common experience but one that can be damaging to your self-esteem and overall well-being.

One way to tackle negative self-talk is to practice positive self-talk. This involves saying nice things to yourself and affirming your own worth and capabilities. Here are some steps to validate yourself through positive self-talk:

- Become aware of your negative self-talk. When you think or say negative things about yourself, pause and take notice.

- Challenge your negative self-talk. Ask yourself if what you're saying is really true, and look for evidence to support or contradict it.

- Once you've challenged your negative self-talk, replace it with positive affirmations. These can be simple statements like "I am worthy" or "I am capable." Repeat these affirmations to yourself throughout the day, or write them down and post them where you can see them.

- Make positive self-talk a habit. Practice saying nice things to yourself every day, and incorporate positive affirmations into your daily routine. With practice and persistence, positive self-talk can become a natural and automatic part of your thought process.

By validating yourself through positive self-talk, you can build self-confidence, improve your self-esteem, and cultivate a more positive and compassionate relationship with yourself. So go ahead, say something nice to yourself today – you deserve it.

Steps to Take to Validate Your Feelings

Validating your feelings isn't something ambiguous as you may think. With these steps, you will be able to validate your feelings. Let's proceed.

Pay attention to your feelings and needs

The first step to validating your feelings is to become aware of your feelings and needs. It might seem obvious, but sometimes we get so busy that we forget to check in with ourselves. So, take a moment to pause and notice how you're feeling. Maybe you're feeling stressed, anxious, or overwhelmed. And what do you need right now? Maybe you need some alone time, a good night's sleep, or a chance to talk to a trusted friend.

Accept your feelings and needs without judgment

Once you've identified your feelings and needs, accepting them without judgment is important. This means acknowledging your feelings and needs are valid and okay, even if they're uncomfortable or inconvenient. You might say, "It's okay to feel stressed right now. And it's okay to need some time to myself to recharge."

Don't identify too closely with your feelings

While it's important to acknowledge and accept your feelings, it's also important not to get too wrapped up in them. Our feelings are a part of us, but they don't define us. So, instead of saying, "I am angry," try saying, "I feel angry." By using this language, you're reminding yourself that your feelings are temporary and that they don't define who you are as a person.

Practice, practice, practice

Finally, remember that validating yourself is a skill that takes practice. You cannot master it overnight. But with time and patience, you can become more skilled at recognizing and validating your feelings. So, make an effort to practice self-validation regularly. Maybe you set aside a few minutes each day to check in with yourself and identify your feelings and needs. Or maybe you practice self-validation when you're feeling overwhelmed or stressed.

In conclusion, validating your emotions is crucial for your well-being. By practicing self-validation, you'll learn to accept and acknowledge your emotions without judgment. Remember, validating your feelings doesn't mean you have to agree with them all the time, but it means that you're giving yourself the space to experience and process them. With practice, you can learn to effectively validate your emotions and lead a happier life.

Key Takeaways

- External validation should not replace self-validation,
- Validating your emotions involves noticing, accepting, and encouraging them without judgment.
- Prioritizing your needs is crucial for self-validation.

- Accepting your limitations, flaws, and mistakes is important to validate your emotions.

- Saying nice things to yourself can boost your self-esteem and help you validate your feelings.

Conclusion

Congratulations! You have taken bold steps in learning how to validate your feelings. You've taken the first step towards acknowledging and accepting your emotions, overcoming self-doubt, and stopping second-guessing yourself for good.

Throughout this book, you have learned what emotions are, how they are formed, and their effects on us in general. You have also learned about the difference between emotions and feelings and how they relate. You have discovered how our emotions are influenced by the people and occurrences around us, and you have learned about the two hemispheres of emotions. With the knowledge you have gained, you will be able to understand why you express some emotions and what to do about them.

For instance, in the chapters on Negative emotions, you learned about the five key emotions that contribute to self-doubt - anger, fear, resentment, frustration, and anxiety. You've seen how these emotions build up in us and their negative impacts and effects.

Interestingly, the focus of this book is on the Right Hemisphere Emotions that can help us overcome self-doubt and build a great life. And, of course, I delivered on my promise of exploring these positive emotions and gaining a deeper insight into them.

In the chapters on right hemisphere emotions, you've learned about the five basic emotions - Love, Serendipity, Forgiveness, Hope, and Pride. You've seen how love is a great emotion that we all need to build a great life. You have also discovered how we can position ourselves to experience serendipity more often.

In addition, you better understand the power of self-forgiveness and forgiveness of others and how it can be instrumental in our ability to take up new tasks. You have also seen the healing capacity of hope and the positive effects it can have on our lives. And finally, you've learned about the positive effect of pride in our lives and how it can help us do more than doubt ourselves.

I am glad that you have learned all these, but if there is one thing, I don't want you to forget, it's the fact that you should focus on the right hemisphere of your emotions and try to do away with negative emotions. Remember that emotions are an important part of who we are and should be acknowledged and accepted. Embrace the positive emotions that can help you overcome self-doubt and build a great life. Love, serendipity, forgiveness, hope, and pride are powerful emotions that can help you live a happy and fulfilled life.

I hope that the effort I put into capturing my thoughts into words has helped you in some way. Remember that it's never too late to start acknowledging and accepting your emotions, overcoming self-doubt, and stopping second-guessing yourself for good. Good luck on your journey to emotional validation!

Resources

Emotion Typology, (2018) "Hope" Retrieved from https://emotiontypology.com/positive_emotion/hope/ Accessed on April 26th, 2023

https://emotiontypology.com/positive_emotion/pride/#:~:text=The%20feeling%20when%20you%20possess,that%20you%20are%20proud%20about. Accessed on April 20th, 2023

Mentalhelp.net, (2020) "Psychology of Anger" Retrieved from https://www.mentalhelp.net/anger/ Accessed on April 25th, 2023

Penn State (2020) " "Two types of pride" PSYCHOLOGY OF HUMAN EMOTION: AN OPEN ACCESS TEXTBOOK" Retrieved from https://psu.pb.unizin.org/psych425/chapter/two-types-of-pride/ accessed on April 25th, 2023

PsychCentral, (2023). "Why Is Hope So Important? (2021) retrieved from https://psychcentral.com/blog/the-psychology-of-hope#tips accessed on April 25th, 2023

Traci Pedersen, (2022) "Why is hope so important" Retrieved from https://psychcentral.com/blog/the-psychology-of-hope#tips Accessed on April 20th, 2023

Web MD editor (2022) "Signs of Resentment" Retrieved from https://www.webmd.com/mental-health/signs-resentment#:~:text=Treating%20Resentment-,What%20Is%20Resentment%3F,a%20normal%20part%20of%20life. Accessed on April 25th, 2023

WebMD Editorial Contributors, (2022) "Signs of Resentment" Retrieved from https://www.webmd.com/mental-health/signs-resentment#:~:text=Treating%20Resentment-,What%20Is%20Resentment%3F,a%20normal%20part%20of%20life. Accessed on April 20th, 2023